The William J. Glackens Collection

The William J. Glackens Collection in the Museum of Art | Fort Lauderdale

ELIZABETH THOMPSON COLLEARY

Museum of Art | Fort Lauderdale

NOVA SOUTHEASTERN UNIVERSITY

Funding for The William J. Glackens Collection in the Museum of Art | Fort Lauderdale has been gener-
ously provided by the Sansom Foundation.

COPY EDITING: Fronia W. Simpson
DESIGN: Michael Russem, Kat Ran Press
PRINTING: GHP Media

Funding for the Museum of Art is provided, in part, by the Broward County Board of County Commission-
ers as recommended by the Broward Cultural Council; the State of Florida, Department of State, Division
of Cultural Affairs; and the Florida Council on Arts and Culture.

CONTENTS

Ira Glackens, not dated. Museum of Art | Fort Lauderdale, Nova Southeastern University;
Bequest of Ira Glackens

Foreword

I first met William Glackens's son, Ira, and his wife, Nancy, in New York in 1973. They were visiting from their home in Shepherdstown, West Virginia, and their financial adviser and close friend, C. Richard Hilker, whom I knew well, suggested we all have dinner together. The Glackenses were in need of a new lawyer.

Ira and Nancy had the reputation of being a bit stern, and to me, as a young attorney, they seemed positively daunting. But it was a lovely dinner, spiced with wonderful conversation, and somehow, we clicked, thus beginning my education on the life and work of the painter William James Glackens and my career-long involvement with the Sansom Foundation.

In 1955 Ira inherited a considerable estate that combined wealth from his mother's side of the family and the works of art created by his father that his mother had carefully saved in the hopes of forming a Glackens museum. Shortly thereafter, Ira and Nancy established the Sansom Foundation to preserve, honor, and foster William Glackens's legacy.

In addition to supporting their charitable interests in art, education, and animal welfare, Ira and Nancy donated works of art to such institutions as the National Gallery of Art, the National Portrait Gallery, the Smithsonian American Art Museum, and the Smith College Museum of Art. They even presented a painting to the White House during the Johnson administration.

Despite his dedication to his father's legacy, Ira was not particularly sentimental, and he rarely spoke about his father or the Eight, although there was always a great deal of conversation concerning art and culture. Of course, that did not at all mean Ira was not an expert on his father's work. One of the first things I did after being retained by Ira and Nancy was to read Ira's book on the Eight, along with everything else he had ever written. The second thing I did was to visit the Metropolitan Museum of Art to see firsthand what I was getting involved with, and I was immediately captivated.

As was the case with so many others, I was charmed by William Glackens's genuine enjoyment of life, so readily evident in his work. He was a superb draftsman whose drawings and sketches captured detail with seeming effortlessness, his hand quick and accurate. In his paintings over the years, the line became broader and more flowing, and the focus shifted from detail to fascination with color. Perhaps because I am a native New Yorker, I am much taken by Glackens's canvases depicting Central Park and Washington Square with its grand arch, in front of which, as a law student at New York University, I used to eat lunch, study, and take in the passing scene.

But my favorite Glackens works are his intimate family portraits, especially *Breakfast Porch* (pl. 18), which so well expresses the love and contentment he felt in the everyday moments of his life. It is not a coincidence that one of my great treasures is a quick sketch in pastel on brown paper of a young boy holding something to his lips—

a spot of white, which my dear friend the art historian Avis Berman pointed out was a teacup, the drawing actually being a study of Ira for *The Breakfast Porch*.

Ira felt very confident about bequeathing a major portion of his father's artistic estate to the Museum of Art | Fort Lauderdale and entrusting curator Jorge Hilker Santis to oversee the care and use of the William J. Glackens Collection with the on-going support and partnership of the Sansom Foundation. Over the years, the Museum's Glackens Collection projects have been substantive, comprising dozens of exhibitions and the construction of the Glackens Wing in 2001. Now, with this comprehensive handbook of the Museum's William J. Glackens Collection, we are poised on the threshold of a new level of scholarship and recognition for the artist.

Among these activities is the Glackens Research Collection and Study Center, a repository both web-based and physical for Glackens materials that establishes the Museum of Art | Fort Lauderdale as a center for scholarship on this important American artist. No less important is the first major survey of the work of William Glackens since 1966 that opened at the Museum of Art | Fort Lauderdale in February 2014. The exhibition *William Glackens* wound its way through some of the artist's old locales, to the Parrish Museum of Art in Water Mill, New York, on Long Island, where the Glackens family spent many summer days enjoying the beaches, and, finally, to the Barnes Foundation in Philadelphia, Pennsylvania, the city in which the artist was born and first began to paint.

I speak on behalf of all of my fellow members of the Board of Directors of the Sansom Foundation when I say that, while the Sansom Foundation has engaged, and continues to engage, in many worthy endeavors, none matches the importance of these initiatives.

And Ira? Well, he would have been enormously pleased with all of this—tributes he himself would have envisioned for his father's work.

Frank M. Buscaglia
President, Sansom Foundation

Director's Statement

When the Museum of Art | Fort Lauderdale merged with Nova Southeastern University in 2008, it placed us at a new institutional threshold that provided a myriad of opportunities to develop our creative campus, enrich our programs, and further our outreach.

Following the merger, the Museum of Art's Board of Governors, under the leadership of then chair of the Strategic Planning Committee, David Horvitz, immediately set to work on a new strategic plan that built on the Museum of Art's mission to actively engage diverse audiences in the appreciation of works of art through innovative exhibition, education, publication, and collection activities along with NSU's long-standing dedication to academic study.

Primary among five transformational goals identified in the plan was the following: to develop an increased understanding of the Museum's collections—the core of our cultural equity—through a new conceptualization of our collecting and exhibition priorities. The pursuit of this goal resulted in an important new endeavor, the Collections Research Initiative, the aim of which has been to strengthen the Museum of Art's collections in four key areas: scholarship, use, access, and engagement.

As one of our primary artistic assets, the Museum of Art's William J. Glackens Collection has been at the leading edge of this initiative. The publication of this handbook on the Museum's William J. Glackens Collection is only one of several such activities.

Another of these is our William J. Glackens Research Collection and Study Center, a web-based and physical resource that will provide a central repository for all current and future Glackens research materials owned by the Museum of Art—works of art, sketchbooks, illustrated books, photographic archives, institutional records, correspondence, exhibition reviews, press releases, and educational materials—and establishes our institution as the definitive place for information on Glackens.

The Museum also organized the first comprehensive survey of the artist's work in nearly fifty years, bringing together more than one hundred of Glackens's most important works from about fifty of America's finest public and private collections. After debuting in Fort Lauderdale, this major exhibition traveled to our coorganizing partners—the Parrish Art Museum in Water Mill, New York, and the Barnes Foundation in Philadelphia, Pennsylvania. Our William J. Glackens Collection initiatives comprise some of the biggest and most exciting endeavors our Museum has ever undertaken, and we are thrilled that our efforts are casting a national spotlight on a significant American artist.

We could not do this without the support of some very important and committed people and organizations. First and foremost, I wish to thank the Sansom Foundation. All of these developments are a direct result of Ira Glackens's donation of works of art by his father and the steadfast support of former Sansom Foundation presidents,

Parlor in the William J. Glackens Wing. This room is a re-creation of the living room in the Glackens family home at 23 Fifth Avenue, New York, c. 1910.

C. Richard Hilker and Donald Hilker, and current Sansom Foundation president, Frank M. Buscaglia, Esq., and Trustees Richard Barrette, Lawrence Thompson, Esq., and Jorge Hilker Santis. Their tireless vision and ongoing commitment are the reasons the Museum of Art's William J. Glackens Collection is now receiving the attention it so well deserves.

I also wish to thank Holly Bodenweber and the Hudson Family Foundation for their support of our collections activities and dedication to the care and conservation of objects in our possession for the lasting enjoyment of our visitors and the benefit of our community.

I want to take this opportunity to thank the many hard-working individuals who have given a great deal of energy and talent toward this publication. In particular, I acknowledge our scholars, Jorge Hilker Santis, Curator at the Museum of Art | Fort Lauderdale, who provides a thoughtful overview of the collection; and Elizabeth Thompson Colleary, who has contributed significant scholarship on the Museum of Art's William J. Glackens Collection. I also want to thank our Director of Exhibitions and Curatorial Services, Rachel Talent Ivers, Registrar of Collections, Rachel Diana, Registrar of Exhibitions, Diana Blanco, and former Registrar of Exhibitions, Stacy Slavichak, for their tireless work on this project. Under their direction, many others have devoted themselves to this endeavor, including former Collections and Records Associate, Carrie Peterson, former Curatorial Research Associate, Emily Wood, and former interns Ben Feldman and Amy Snitehurst. Michael Russem of Kat Ran Press is

Gallery view, The William J. Glackens Wing, showing *Portrait of Charles FitzGerald* (1903) and *Dancer in Blue* (c. 1906)

responsible for the elegant design of this publication, which is sure to be an indispensable guide for our Museum of Art for many years to come.

My special thanks go to the Museum of Art's leadership team, including former Executive Director Irvin Lippman and Interim Director William R. Stanton, whose guidance has been critical for the development of our Collections Research Initiatives.

Finally, I wish to express my gratitude to Dr. George L. Hanbury II, President and Chief Executive Officer of NSU, the University's Board of Trustees, and the Museum of Art's Board of Governors, in particular our current chair, David Horvitz, and immediate past chair, Mike Jackson, for their ongoing service and unwavering commitment to our mission and our core values, which are perfectly embodied in our Collections Research Initiatives.

This publication is envisioned as the first in a series of volumes on the Museum of Art | Fort Lauderdale's collections. As we shape our permanent holdings in ways that are increasingly accessible, relevant, and meaningful to our community, we expand the prominence and importance of our Museum of Art as an educational and cultural resource for the twenty-first century.

Bonnie Clearwater
Director and Chief Curator
Museum of Art | Fort Lauderdale
Nova Southeastern University

Girl with a Green Apple, c. 1911
Oil on canvas. 26 × 32 inches. Museum of Art |
Fort Lauderdale, Nova Southeastern University;
Gift of the Sansom Foundation. 2013.4

The Significance of the Glackens Collection

On February 28, 2001, the Museum of Art | Fort Lauderdale, Nova Southeastern University inaugurated a new wing with fanfare and a stunning exhibition of works by the Philadelphia artist William J. Glackens (see page 11), which came to the museum through a bequest from Ira Glackens, the artist's son. The artistic merit of the Glackens Collection is immeasurable; it provides Museum visitors and scholars with a panoramic view of Glackens's oeuvre. A glance at the Museum's extensive holdings allows us to grasp the painter's propensity to incorporate into his artistic output rich influences from such masters as Frans Hals, Édouard Manet, Pierre-Auguste Renoir, and Henri Matisse.

Thematically, the collection is rich and varied. Its more than thirteen hundred objects include illustrations of episodes from the Spanish-American War as well as paintings of colorful romantic Parisian vignettes. Glackens, always interested in the world around him, recorded bustling streets in New York City, where he lived, and scenic views of the places he vacationed with his family in New England and in various locales in France. The range of media he used is broad, encompassing pencil, crayon, pen and ink, watercolor, oil paint, etching, lithography, and photogravure.

In addition to oil paintings by Glackens, the collection includes graphics and canvases by some of his closest friends and best-known colleagues, among them John Sloan and Maurice Prendergast. Works by his immediate (and talented) family add to the depth of the collection: drawings by his older brother Louis, a noted magazine illustrator; and a few oils and drawings by his beloved daughter, Lenna. An exemplary collection of works by Glackens's wife, Edith Dimock Glackens, is significant. She was an established watercolorist who had studied with the acclaimed American Impressionist painter William Merritt Chase and had exhibited her work, both before and after marriage, in prestigious exhibitions, among them the Armory Show in 1913. Because later in life Edith destroyed many of her own works, those in the Museum's collection are now all the more precious as documents of her achievement.

The comprehensiveness of the Glackens Collection makes it an invaluable resource. The artist's seventy-seven sketchbooks are essential tools for confirming attributions of Glackens's works. Furthermore, they provide an intimate glimpse into how the artist arrived at his most elemental artistic decisions. Moreover, the creation, survival, and growth of the Glackens Collection fulfilled the dream of a devoted widow whose aim was to honor her husband's artistic legacy in perpetuity.

For twenty-four years, the Hartford-born watercolorist Edith Dimock was happily married to William Glackens. From their union, two offspring were born: Ira (1907–1990) and Lenna (1913–1942). According to Ira, his mother's world revolved around his father; Edith's main objective was to provide her mate with a tranquil environment in which to create art. To achieve her goal, Edith often neglected her own artistic career

Ira and Nancy Glackens with dog, Lucifer, seated beneath *Family Group*, not dated. Museum of Art | Fort Lauderdale, Nova Southeastern University; Bequest of Ira Glackens

to run a busy household, which included making arrangements for the family's extensive foreign travel. William's sudden death from a brain hemorrhage in 1938 prompted her to make decisions that had long-lasting ramifications: she suspended the sale of Glackens's works so that they could be rotated indefinitely as a makeshift memorial in an annual exhibition held in their Greenwich Village home, dedicated to his artistic legacy. She also embraced mourning, declaring that she would never wear color again. After 1949, though, Edith's noble intent was abandoned. Six years later, in 1955, she, too, passed away, and her portion of William's painting inventory went to their son, Ira, who had inherited Lenna's share thirteen years earlier.

In the spring of 1990, Nancy Gracie Middlebrook, Ira's wife, died childless and without any close relatives. Ira, now a widower and very much aware of his own mortality, was forced to make decisions regarding his assets, which included real estate, a portfolio of stocks, and a large trove of artwork. C. Richard Hilker (1925–2001), Ira's friend and personal business consultant, suggested that his art collection be given to a museum to avoid onerous estate duties. At first, large institutions such as the National Gallery of Art and the Hirshhorn Museum and Sculpture Garden, both in Washington, D.C., showed interest, but their unwillingness to agree to Ira's wish that a portion of the future bequest be kept permanently on view forced Ira to search elsewhere. At the time, Hilker was a board member of the Museum of Art | Fort Lauderdale, and he proposed that this south Florida venue be considered. Several months later, Ira rewrote his will, and in it he bequeathed his permanent collection to our Museum. Following Ira's death, in November 1990, Hilker became president of the Sansom Foundation, which Ira and his wife had founded in the 1950s and named after the street in Philadelphia where William Glackens was born. This nonprofit foundation controls the remainder of Glackens's extensive inventory of art. As head of the Sansom Foundation,

Philadelphia Landscape, 1893. Oil on canvas. 17¾ × 24 inches. Museum of Art | Fort Lauderdale, Nova Southeastern University; Gift of the Sansom Foundation. 92.41

Hilker not only added three hundred more works to the Museum's collection, including seventy-seven of Glackens's sketchbooks, but the Sansom Foundation also donated more than one million dollars to build what is known today as the Glackens Wing, a ten-thousand-square-foot addition to the Museum of Art | Fort Lauderdale, which, as noted, opened in 2001. Since then, it has been used to present exhibitions that explore in depth various aspects of his oeuvre, while at the same time showcasing the works of his fellow Ashcan artists. In so doing, the Glackens Collection and the Glackens Wing at the Museum of Art | Fort Lauderdale proudly advance our understanding of and appreciation for early twentieth-century American art.

Jorge Hilker Santis
Curator
Museum of Art | Fort Lauderdale
Nova Southeastern University

William J. Glackens painting *Tulips*, winner of the
Allegheny Garden Club Prize, Carnegie International
Exhibition, 1936. Museum of Art | Fort Lauderdale,
Nova Southeastern University; Bequest of Ira Glackens

ELIZABETH THOMPSON COLLEARY

Highlights from the Glackens Collection

> Every time a group of paintings by William Glackens is shown one gets from them much of the sensuous joy that the artist must evidently have had when he painted them. His are no perfunctory productions of a manufacturer of paintings. They are fragments of his life, of the pleasures he has felt at being in the sun in certain delightful places and above all of the pleasure derived from just painting.[1]

Written by an art critic reviewing an exhibition of paintings in 1931 by William J. Glackens (1870–1938), this statement aptly describes the experience that awaits visitors to the Glackens Wing at the Museum of Art | Fort Lauderdale. As the largest repository of resplendent works by the artist, recently described as a "master of delight" and praised in his lifetime for "his genius for transforming his inner joyousness to canvas,"[2] the collection includes paintings spanning the years 1891 to 1938, thus from the defining phases of Glackens's career—from his early days as an artist-reporter and illustrator, through his recognition as an urban realist aligned with the famed painter and teacher Robert Henri, to his brilliant flowering when he came into his own, inspired by the vivid colors of the French Impressionists and his American modernist contemporaries.

Among the holdings are examples of his finest works as an illustrator, among them *The Night after San Juan* (1898; pl. 2), which depicts the aftermath of a battle in the Spanish-American War, *Far from the Fresh Air Farm* (1911; pl. 8), and *Christmas Shoppers, Madison Square* (1912; pl. 9), the latter two bustling New York City street scenes replete with lively vignettes and abundant period detail. He was considered by many to be one of the best, if not the best, illustrator of his generation, and, although the drawings were originally created for reproduction in magazines, they are now regarded as independent works of art of the highest order.

Always intent on pursuing a career as an artist, Glackens took classes at the Pennsylvania Academy of the Fine Arts and shared a studio with Henri (fig. 1). Although he was earning a living as an illustrator, he was nonetheless determined to make his way as a painter, and, to complete his education, he traveled to Europe in 1895–1896 with Henri to study the works of the masters he revered. He was enthralled by the paintings of Rembrandt van Rijn and Frans Hals, the seventeenth-century artists whose works he saw in Holland, and in Paris he discovered the paintings of Édouard Manet, whose influence is evident in *In the Luxembourg* (c. 1896). Glackens's passion for French art and culture first emerged in Paris; he remained an ardent Francophile for the rest of his life, returning to France often for extended vacations with his family. A few of his most vibrant paintings, completed in that country after his conversion to a more colorful Impressionist palette, are in the Museum of Art | Fort Lauderdale collection, among them *Breakfast Porch* and *Along the Marne* (both 1925) and *Bowlers, La Ciotat* (1930) and *Bayshore* (1931), the last painted during his final summer in France.

Fig. 1 William Glackens with Robert Henri, c. 1905. Museum of Art | Fort Lauderdale, Nova Southeastern University; Bequest of Ira Glackens

After Glackens moved to New York City in 1896, he worked for numerous publications as an illustrator before he began to exhibit his paintings in 1901. His career was given a boost by the *New York Evening Sun* art critic Charles FitzGerald, an early champion of his work who was immortalized by Glackens in a handsome full-length portrait dating from 1903 (pl. 3). FitzGerald became a good friend and later a brother-in-law, when he married Glackens's wife's sister after meeting her at Glackens's wedding.

In 1904 Glackens married Edith Dimock, a spirited and freethinking artist from a wealthy Connecticut family (fig. 2). They met through a mutual friend when she was living in New York City and studying with the American Impressionist painter William Merritt Chase. Some of her lively and satirical watercolors are in the Museum of Art | Fort Lauderdale collection as well, and although she downplayed her achievements as a painter, her work was included in the groundbreaking Armory Show of 1913 that featured European and American modern art, much of it shown in the United States for the first time. Glackens's work was also on view in the exhibition, and the leadership role he assumed in helping to organize it is an indication of his stature within the New York City art community.

When Glackens and his new bride took a delayed honeymoon to France in 1906, he once again saw the works of the Impressionists, and the experience marked the beginning of his conversion to a brighter palette—*Dancer in Blue* (c. 1906) signals the new coloristic style to come. Glackens first gained notoriety in 1908, when he and fellow

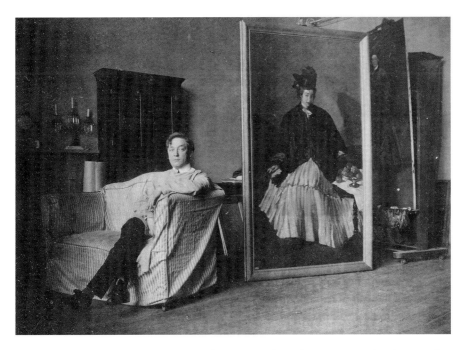

Fig. 2 William Glackens seated with *Portrait of the Artist's Wife*, not dated. Museum of Art | Fort Lauderdale, Nova Southeastern University; Bequest of Ira Glackens

urban realist painters organized the now historic exhibition of the Eight, yet he soon moved away from the darker style of Henri and Manet.

After his marriage and the birth of his children, Glackens's subjects were often drawn from the parks and beaches the family visited—*Cape Cod Pier* (1908) and *Sledding in Central Park* (1912) among them—and interior views of the places they lived—including *Twenty-Three Fifth Avenue, Interior* (1910) and *Artist's Daughter in Chinese Costume* (1918). All rendered with sonorous color and feathered brushwork, they reflect what has been described as "a communion between the painter and his subject," with an emphasis on "the contemplation of … joy."[3]

Glackens's connoisseurship, discerning taste, and critical eye were admired and valued by Dr. Albert Barnes, a boyhood friend from Philadelphia who contacted Glackens after he had amassed a fortune and developed a passion for modern art (fig. 3). He sought out his learned friend's advice when he began to build his art collection, now one of the most acclaimed in the world. One of the treasures of the Museum of Art | Fort Lauderdale collection is a small notebook Glackens kept while in Europe on an art-buying trip, shopping for Barnes—it includes the names of such modern masters as Vincent van Gogh, Pierre-Auguste Renoir, Paul Gauguin, and Henri Matisse and lists prices for their works that Glackens had negotiated with art dealers. Dr. Barnes was also one of Glackens's most enthusiastic patrons, buying pictures from the artist

Fig. 3 Dr. Albert Barnes (left) with William Glackens, not dated. Museum of Art | Fort Lauderdale, Nova Southeastern University; Bequest of Ira Glackens

regularly; the Barnes Foundation owns more than seventy works by Glackens, a collection second in size only to that of the one at the Museum of Art | Fort Lauderdale.

Toward the end of his life, through the 1930s, when his health was failing and he lacked the physical stamina required to paint larger works, Glackens focused primarily on still-life subjects—the paintings were popular in his lifetime and are now considered among his finest. As early as 1904 in figurative paintings, Glackens had featured colorful still-life arrangements of flowers and fruit, often depictions of objects found in his home, and by 1916 he began to exhibit still lifes that displayed the bold palette and lively brushwork of his new Impressionist style—examples include *Flowers on a Garden Chair* (1925; pl. 23), *Plums in a Saucer* (c. 1930s; pl. 24), and *Flowers in a Quimper Pitcher* (c. 1930; pl. 25). The last painting that Glackens produced, a small still life with paint tubes (1937–1938; pl. 28), is a simple arrangement he came upon in his studio, three casually placed paint tubes and a small bottle of turpentine or linseed oil—a poignant evocation of the decades he had spent sharing with his viewers "the pleasure derived from just painting."

In retrospect, the observations made at the time of Glackens's death regarding his place in the pantheon of American art, still ring true today. On the occasion of the large retrospective memorial exhibition mounted at the Whitney Museum of American Art, New York, shortly after his death, Glackens's stature was recognized by a critic who wrote with obvious affection, admiration, and respect that "the artist, with his freshness and serenity of vision, his command over the possibilities of color, his ability to weave light and form into one motive, and his genius for transforming his inner joyousness to canvas through flowers, landscapes and figures, found a place—a very high place, unsought but earned—in the history of American art."[4]

Commentaries on Selected Works

1 In the Luxembourg, c. 1896

Oil on canvas. 16 × 19 inches. Bequest of Ira Glackens. 91.40.66

In the Luxembourg was painted in Paris during Glackens's first trip to the city, an extended sojourn with a group of fellow artists, most notably Robert Henri. Unlike other painters who went to Europe to study, Glackens did not enroll in classes; he preferred to sketch local views and study the art on display in museums. During a biking trip to Holland, he saw the paintings of the much-esteemed seventeenth-century Dutch painters Frans Hals and Rembrandt van Rijn, and their emphasis on loose brushwork and dramatic light clearly influenced Glackens during these formative years. If Glackens's painterly style was derivative of seventeenth-century Dutch art, the subjects of the paintings from this period were clearly inspired by the earlier work of the Impressionists and other painters of modern life. Like them, Glackens favored views of Parisian parks, cafés, and theaters showing people taking their ease.

Glackens most admired the works of Édouard Manet and Pierre-Auguste Renoir, and while *In the Luxembourg* may in conception be similar to such works as Manet's *La Musique aux Tuileries* of 1862 (The National Gallery, London) and Renoir's *Bal du Moulin de la Galette* of 1876 (Musée d'Orsay, Paris), the treatment of the subject—people in a park setting—could not be more different. The foreground space in Manet's painting is densely packed with figures and wrought-iron chairs, arranged in a composition that mimics a friezelike tableau, and Renoir's painting features a similarly crowded foreground scene. In Glackens's composition the relatively passive figures of the Frenchmen, seated side by side in the shallow foreground plane, have been replaced with a few children playing in the distance and an open expanse of foreground, in which a single female figure rushes toward the viewer. Unlike the works by Manet and Renoir, in Glackens's painting the space opens out to the viewer, and the figure about to sweep by, her skirts hiked up so she can move quickly, suggests a narrative. By placing her prominently in an expansive foreground, Glackens makes her, and whatever story her presence and demeanor may suggest, the focus of the painting. Clearly, in this early work the artist-reporter's gift for careful, nuanced observation of the human condition in all its various aspects emerges, as does his desire for the viewer to become engaged with the narrative.

This contemporary subject in a setting replete with not only the lone rushing figure but also numerous children at play is presented in an earth-toned palette and with loose brushwork that are clearly derivative of Hals and Manet. In the paint strokes that describe the mists of water spraying from the fountain in the distance, the impasto used in the clouds above, and the thickly dappled strokes of paint that define the simplified forms of the smaller figures, Glackens has fully embraced the style of the earlier masters.

2 The Night after San Juan, 1898

Watercolor, pen, and black ink on paper. 16 × 13 inches. Bequest of Ira Glackens. 91.40.67

From 1891 to 1895 Glackens worked as an artist-reporter in Philadelphia. Then he stayed in Europe for more than a year before moving to New York City late in 1896 to pursue a career as an illustrator; illustration work provided income for the next twenty-three years. The years 1899 through 1906 were his most active; he created illustrations for more than 160 articles and a dozen books.[5] Throughout his life, even after he had gained recognition and acclaim as a painter, he continued to be praised not only for his skill as a draftsman but for "his truth to tell" as an illustrator and "his sincerity in telling it."[6] He was also much admired by his fellow artists for his virtuosity. Everett Shinn, for example, once touted his friend, stating, "William J. Glackens is the greatest draughtsman this country has produced."[7]

Hiring himself out to different newspapers and magazines, Glackens also worked as a cartoonist, creating humorous drawings for the *New York Sunday World*, and as an artist-reporter at the *New York Herald*, where he went "to news-making events … to draw a variety of subjects for daily publication, from fires and murders to high-society events and political speeches."[8] After 1898 Glackens found employment as a freelance illustrator, most often creating drawings to accompany works of fiction. He also produced independent illustrations that were neither inspired by nor related to written sources. These were among his most popular works, admired when they appeared in magazines and enjoyed now as singular, exemplary works of art.

Among Glackens's most highly regarded illustrations are those that he created while covering the Spanish-American War in Havana, Cuba, as a special correspondent for *McClures's Magazine*; this was the last artist-reporter assignment that he accepted. Before departing for Cuba, he received "detailed instructions from the manager of McClures's art department," stating that he was "to go to Cuba with the American troops and send back illustrations telling the story of the departures, voyage and arrival, and subsequent work and fights of the U.S. troops."[9] Although twenty-two of Glackens's illustrations were published, when the war ended abruptly, the remaining drawings, more than twenty, were not, among them works that are now considered some of his finest, including *The Night after San Juan*. The battle that became known as the Battle of San Juan Hill was a decisive one, famous for the American victory secured by Theodore Roosevelt serving as the commander of the Rough Riders. Later heralded as a glorious American victory, casualties were nonetheless heavy, and Glackens chose to illustrate the brutality of the conflict. The somber colors, necessary for illustration work, add to the gloominess of the scene, and, although accurately rendering what the artist observed, the rough, agitated surface of the drawing adds to the emotional pitch.

As he would so often do, to engage the emotions of the viewer, Glackens used an expansive foreground to make fully visible the horrors of the story as it unfolded—figures move toward us, and the injured soldier on the right, supported by two comrades, looks as if he will drop at our feet. Behind this group, two soldiers dash to the

left with weapons drawn, advancing toward an unseen enemy, and slain soldiers are in plain sight. The white uniform of the fallen soldier in the left foreground is especially jarring because it draws our eye to his corpse and the twisted body of the dead soldier behind him—by painting them in stark values Glackens highlighted these victims of war. Another patch of lighter pigment is used on the drooping head and neck of the wounded soldier in the right foreground. He is closest and therefore most visible to the viewer, and clearly Glackens wanted us to take direct note of his suffering. This slumping, nearly fallen man expresses the despair that all present at the scene, including the artist-reporter, no doubt felt when witnessing the carnage of this battle. Since Glackens's assignment was to illustrate the "work and fights of the U.S. troops in Cuba," he has done so in an emotionally compelling fashion.

Almost fifty years after the illustration was created, *The Night after San Juan* was still recognized as representing Glackens's best efforts in his early artist-reporter days when, in 1945, it was included in the exhibition *Artists of the Philadelphia Press* at the Philadelphia Museum of Art. The exhibition, which also included Glackens's famous and highly regarded oil painting *At Mouquin's* of 1905 (see fig. 5, p. 32), was reviewed in *Time* magazine in an article entitled "The Press: Reporters of the Brush." There the critic praised *The Night after San Juan* as "a topflight demonstration of vivid, accurate reporting."[10] Even though Glackens's San Juan illustrations were intended for reproduction in a magazine, they have been appreciated as independent works of art and shown in fine art exhibitions to wide acclaim. Works from *The Night after San Juan* series were included in the exhibitions *American Battle Painting: 1776–1918* at the Museum of Modern Art in New York in 1944 and *American Procession, 1492–1900* at the Corcoran Gallery of Art in Washington, D.C, in 1950. A *Time* magazine review of the Corcoran show noted that while the exhibition, "the liveliest art show the capital had seen in many months," was "big and rambling … there was some good art," including "William Glackens' moving paintings of the Spanish-American war."[11]

3 Portrait of Charles FitzGerald, 1903

Oil on canvas. 73¼ × 40 inches. Gift of the Sansom Foundation. 92.45

In 1901, two years before this elegant and flattering portrait was completed, Charles FitzGerald (1873–1958), the recently appointed art critic for the *New York Evening Sun*, had given Glackens his first substantive review. In it he proclaimed the artist "one of the very few illustrators in this country whose work deserves serious consideration. In this field he stands as an artist of pronounced individuality, and the work that he shows here reveals him as a painter, too, of more than ordinary ability." FitzGerald's insights into Glackens's early work identified those qualities for which his drawings and paintings would come to be most valued when he described the artist as having

"an interest in the life around him and an observation that are rare enough to deserve attention. Where among the perennials of our regular exhibitions are we to look for a more lively interest in humanity?"[12] FitzGerald soon became a lifelong friend as well as brother-in-law, when he married Glackens's wife's sister, Irene Dimock, eleven years after he met her at Glackens's wedding.

FitzGerald, who was born in Dublin and educated at Trinity College there, was described by Ira Glackens as "so polite, so urbane … he spoke the charming English of Dublin, wore a cape, and had a fine Irish head.… Though he lived thirty years in New York, no one would have known it, for he remained a native of Dublin in look and speech."[13]

When this painting was first exhibited, it was readily identified as owing a debt to comparable full-length portraits by James McNeill Whistler.[14] While employing the same dark tonalities that Whistler favored in his treatment of FitzGerald's clothing and the darkened room he occupies, Glackens draws the viewer's attention to FitzGerald's face by painting his collar a brilliant white and masterfully modeling his head with subtle highlights and shadows. The illumination reveals a superb likeness, and, despite the dominant brown and gray hues, Glackens's penchant for strong color is evident in the faint rose tones in the face and the bright red that colors FitzGerald's full mouth.

FitzGerald does not make eye contact with the viewer; rather, he seems caught in a pensive moment as he glances to the left with a knowing gaze that suggests the thoughtful intelligence that was a hallmark of his character. Glackens faintly illuminated FitzGerald's wrist to draw our attention to his right hand, placed confidently on his hip; his left hand grasps the hat and walking stick that complete his fashionable ensemble. In his attire and stance, he appears a dapper gentleman, proud but not haughty. The vague, dark setting, with no clear floor line or interior details, and the deep, earth-toned palette may have been inspired by the formal concerns of Whistler, but Glackens used them expressively to suggest the contemplative mood of his subject.

4 Tugboat and Lighter, 1904–1905

Oil on canvas. 25 × 30 inches. Bequest of Ira Glackens. 91.40.154

Tugboat and Lighter is an early work that displays the earth-toned palette that Glackens favored at the time, in this case, to capture the energy of the bustling New York harbor views that he often observed. The dynamism of the scene is conveyed through the quickness of the brushstrokes, and the surface is enlivened by layers of paint that accurately describe the play of light and shadow on the boats and water.

The painting is noteworthy as an example of Glackens's early painting technique, and while faithful pictorial definition was clearly a priority, his passion for the spontaneous process of painting can be seen in the diversity of surface textures. The sky is painted

with thin pigment, almost an oil wash, but applied so vigorously that numerous hairs from the paintbrush were dislodged and are still affixed to the canvas. After creating the illusion of a foggy or misty horizon, where the Statue of Liberty can be seen in hazy silhouette, Glackens gradually applied thicker paint in shorter dashing strokes, illusionistically building up the surface in the foreground. The animated gesture of the artist's hand is everywhere visible, especially in the thick impasto that describes the water churning around the boats and the billowing smoke rising from the tugboat. As in the paintings of the French Impressionists whom he would later emulate, here the touch of the artist's brush captures the fleeting reflections of light and shadow on sky and water.

The gold frame on *Tugboat and Lighter* is of interest because it was made by one of Glackens's closest friends. The frame, which is elaborately hand-carved and decorated with scrolling floral motifs incised at the corners (fig. 4), is inscribed on the back: "Frame made for W. Glackens by Charles Prendergast 1917." Charles Prendergast and his brother, Maurice, a fellow member of the group that exhibited as the Eight, became lifelong friends of Glackens, at one point living in the same studio building that Glackens occupied on Washington Square South. The brothers, who began their frame business in Boston at the turn of the twentieth century, are credited with "the

Fig. 4 *Tugboat and Lighter*, detail showing corner of frame

most significant development in American frame design—the return to hand-carved frames … at the vanguard of the change in frame-making was Charles Prendergast."[15] This renewed interest in handcrafting was inspired by the Arts and Crafts movement, which had originated in England as a "reaction to the decline in craftsmanship and the dehumanization of labor which accompanied the Industrial Revolution."[16] The Prendergasts also framed many of the modern works in the Barnes Collection and inspired Glackens to carve some frames of his own.

5 Dancer in Blue, c. 1906

Oil on canvas. 48 × 30 inches. Gift of the Sansom Foundation. 92.43

This painting is now entitled *Dancer in Blue*, but in the card file of detailed information that Ira Glackens kept about his father's paintings, it was also referred to as "Miss K of the Chorus," and the card description reads, "raising skirts above knee."[17] An enigmatic work, *Dancer in Blue* nonetheless displays similarities in style and subject to Glackens's early masterwork *At Mouquin's*, which was painted at the same time and became his most highly acclaimed and widely exhibited work (fig. 5). The paintings are similar in size (both are four feet high, and *At Mouquin's* is only six inches wider), and both highlight blue satin dresses and draw attention to the demeanor, psychology, and personality of the women who wear them. Indeed, a description of the woman in the famous *At Mouquin's* is easily applicable to the young *Dancer in Blue* as well: "she is … visually arresting … her vivid blue dress painted with a confident bravura and creamy texture."[18]

Fig. 5 *At Mouquin's,* 1905
Oil on canvas. 48⅛ × 36¼ inches.
Friends of American Art Collection,
1925.295, The Art Institute of
Chicago. Photography © The Art
Institute of Chicago

The paintings also represent Glackens's early forays into urban nightlife subjects, people enjoying leisure time in interior settings. Since both paintings were done at a time when Glackens was still primarily using a darker palette, they can be seen as pivotal transitional works that represent the direction that Glackens's art would soon take when he wholeheartedly embraced the Impressionist style, especially its colorism. When visiting Paris in 1895–1896, Glackens had seen Impressionist paintings, along with the work of Édouard Manet, and both were a source of inspiration in style and the choice of modern, urban subjects.

Despite their similar lush blue satin dresses, the women in Glackens's two paintings are clearly not the same. The woman in *At Mouquin's* is stationary, seated next to her companion, and looks glum or forlorn. By contrast, the young woman in *Dancer in Blue* is actively in motion, caught midstride as she raises her dress provocatively. And, unlike her counterpart, who gazes to the side, the dancer makes eye contact with the viewer, and with her bright red lips turned up slightly to suggest a tentative smile, this winsome yet vivacious young woman betrays a hint of her character and personality.

The woman's gesture suggests a dance movement, perhaps the cancan, a popular cabaret performance that originated in France, in which performers, wearing long, full skirts, elaborate petticoats, and black stockings and standing in a chorus line, lifted their skirts seductively. Given Glackens's passion for modern French painters, the subject might have been inspired by Henri de Toulouse-Lautrec's many depictions of the popular cancan dancers Jane Avril and Louise Weber (known as La Goulue), who performed at the Moulin Rouge in Paris. The pose seen in *Dancer in Blue*—striding to the side—refers to a cancan performance in which the chorus line moves in precise unison. When first performed at dance halls in Paris, the cancan was considered scandalous because it was danced by courtesans. That disapprobation carried over to the exhibition of *At Mouquin's* in New York and Chicago in 1908: "[C]ritics perceived this picture as 'sensational' and 'vulgar,' focusing on its candid depiction of drinking."[19]

The vibrant blue hues signal Glackens's innate passion for the rich color embraced by the Impressionists, but in both paintings, the dynamic brushwork is reminiscent of Frans Hals, the seventeenth-century Dutch painter whose work had so captivated Glackens when he saw it in Holland in 1896. The "confident bravura and creamy texture" that characterize the application of pigment in *At Mouquin's* are everywhere in evidence in *Dancer in Blue*. Like Hals's, Glackens's brushstrokes are varied and animated. Thick blue and gray strokes fly loosely downward to depict cascading folds of fabric, shorter dashes of white suggest the lace ruffles of the petticoat and neckline, and small softer strokes emulate the porcelain texture of the dancer's skin.

Glackens's abundant enthusiasm for the process of painting can be seen in the active surface of the canvas. The lively motion of his brush, mimicking the movement of the dancer, captures the verve of this young performer while just as emphatically capturing the artist's passion for his work.

6 Study for "Flying Kites, Montmartre," 1906

Oil on panel. 6 × 8 inches. Bequest of Ira Glackens. 91.40.1

After opening in New York City at the Macbeth Gallery in February 1908, the famed exhibition of paintings by the Eight traveled to nine cities around the country for more than a year. Although the roster of artists remained the same, at some venues the selection of paintings varied. The December 1908 catalogue from the Detroit Museum of Art for the exhibition *Paintings by Eight American Artists Resident in New York and Boston* (which misspelled Glackens's name as "William J. Glackins" on the cover) listed six of the same works that had been shown at the Macbeth Gallery version of the show in New York, but *Brighton Beach, Race Track* had been replaced by *Montmartre, Sunday Afternoon*, which, given Glackens's habit of using different descriptive titles for the same work, may well have been *Flying Kites, Montmartre*, the larger oil painting that was based on this study (fig. 6). Curiously, "[t]he only city in which the show received vehement negative coverage was Detroit.... the critic for the *Detroit Free Press* ... denounced the exhibition for its 'puzzling and freakish attempts at bold and defiant realism.' Yet even [this] severe ... critic ... singled out William Glackens's paintings for praise."[20]

The study was painted when Glackens was in Paris with his new bride for a delayed honeymoon. Ira Glackens explained that to his father

> Paris was—Paris! W. had not seen it since 1896. Paris was always my father's favorite city, and France his spiritual home. Everything suited him there, the food, the wine, the people in the streets and public gardens, whom he loved to sketch; the look of restaurants, shops, and cafés; the color of the houses, the signs, the trees, the rivers, the fishermen, the villages, the flow of life. No other country seemed so to invite his pencil and his brush.... They settled down in a studio at 9 rue de Falguière. This address is a court called "Villa Gabrielle" surrounded with

Fig. 6
Flying Kites, Montmartre, 1906.
Oil on canvas. 23¾ × 32 inches.
Museum of Fine Arts, Boston,
The Hayden Collection–Charles
Henry Hayden Fund. 38.7.
Photograph © 2013 Museum
of Fine Arts, Boston

studio buildings.... Alfy Maurer [Alfred Maurer] also had a studio at the Villa Gabrielle and the G.'s went down to Chezy-sur-Marne where the cheerful Alfy had a cottage.... The paintings W.G. brought back from rue Falguière also included "Flying Kites, Montmartre."[21]

Although many of Glackens's pictures of people enjoying leisure time take place in outdoor park settings, in *Study for "Flying Kites, Montmartre"* his subject is recreation in a crowded urban locale. The setting may lack the picturesque beauty of a formal park filled with trees, gardens, and fountains, but Glackens nonetheless conveys the warmth and gaiety of the shared kite-flying experience through the use of radiant light. The most evocative feature of this charming and intimate work is the use of pure white and golden yellow highlights to create the illusion of late afternoon sunlight illuminating the middle ground and buildings in the distance.

Study for "Flying Kites, Montmartre" also displays Glackens's mastery at rendering figures both posing gracefully and in motion. The people seen in silhouette in the right foreground are painted with a few small, quick strokes of black paint, yet, despite the shorthand simplification, they are thoroughly convincing. They stand or move with clearly articulated gestures—the kite-flying figure on the right wearing a red cap pulls back dramatically as he maneuvers his kite string, while a woman next to the lamppost leans to the left, perhaps balancing a baby on her hip. An older man with a cane or walking stick in the lower left corner takes in the scene. Since his back is to us, we are invited to look over his shoulder as we observe the view that he enjoys.

7 Curb Exchange [No. 3], 1907–1910

Gouache and conté crayon. 26½ × 18 inches. Gift of the Sansom Foundation. 92.44

Curb Exchange [No. 3] is among the finest of Glackens's drawings. Although it was not published, "Glackens probably intended it to be, given its similarity in composition and medium to his other published drawings and the fact that he had previously published impressions of Wall Street in *Munsey's Magazine* in 1899, including a scene of curb brokers in front of the stock exchange on Broad Street."[22] It is comparable in subject and style to others that appeared in popular magazines such as *Collier's*, often views of New York City streets teeming with activity and a broad cast of carefully observed characters drawn from the crowds Glackens saw every day.[23]

Glackens produced three versions of this drawing. *Curb Exchange [No. 1]* is owned by the Georgia Museum of Art (fig. 7), and the second is in a private collection. *Curb Exchange [No. 3]* records transactions taking place in lower Manhattan on Broad and Wall Streets, where brokers who did not have seats on the New York Stock Exchange conducted business. As in so many of Glackens's illustrations of urban life, *Curb*

Fig. 7 *Curb Exchange [No. 1]*, 1907–1910. Carbon pencil, watercolor, and Chinese white on paper. 24⅝ × 19³⁄₁₆ inches. Georgia Museum of Art, University of Georgia; University purchase. GMOA 1976.3449

Fig. 8 *Curb Exchange [No. 3]*, detail showing woman selling apples

Exchange [No. 3] features many animated figures presented in narrative vignettes with the activities of those in the foreground emphasized for our most complete attention.

The title refers to the exchange taking place between the male stock traders on the street, yet it could just as easily refer to the woman selling apples from a basket in the foreground (fig. 8). Indeed, given her size and placement in the front, this woman selling two apples to a boy is the most prominent "curb exchange"—and perhaps a humorous play on words on Glackens's part. The negotiation over price is defined by hand gestures: the vendor holds up three fingers, while the messenger boy making the purchase holds up two. In *Curb Exchange [No. 1]*, a second, smaller woman selling fruit from a basket is even more prominent in the center foreground owing to the open space surrounding her and the businessman placing coins in her hand. This same smaller fruit vendor at the left appears in *Curb Exchange [No. 3]*, but here, rather than making a sale, she appears withdrawn, her arms folded tight and her head down, perhaps distressed that customers have passed her by.

To the left of the fruit vendor in *Curb Exchange [No. 3]*, two men are seen in exaggerated poses—one man pleading with another, almost knocking him over as he firmly pokes his shoulder. Behind these men in the foreground, a dense mass of animated figures, mostly men, are depicted. They conduct business while arguing and gesturing dramatically amid this crushing throng. These figures would be lost in a sea of gray hues were it not for Glackens's skillful use of dashes of red on the caps of the two men at the center. The red-capped figures in the center catch the viewer's eye and move it from the action at the front through the crowd back to the end of the street, where the carriage turns away.

In *Curb Exchange [No. 3]*, Glackens employed a favored vertical compositional structure, with smaller figures above or off in the distance and the center of activity tumbling forward. This tightly compressed space, densely packed with figures bustling about in frenetic activity, opens out into the viewer's space in the foreground so we can once again feel part of the scene. Also, in *Curb Exchange [No. 3]*, as he did in many compositions, "Glackens employed an elevated perspective that ... avoids the overlapping of foreground and background," so that while the scene is crowded, the use of raised perspective allows for unobstructed views of figures in the middle ground and background.[24]

Unlike the earlier *McClure's* San Juan illustration, executed in a more painterly style using watercolor and pen and ink (see pl. 2), *Curb Exchange [No. 3]* was drawn using gouache and conté crayon, a drawing medium Glackens preferred. The crayon allowed for much greater emphasis on the animated line that was a hallmark of his style, with abundant agitated cross-hatching that enlivens the surfaces, be they the folds of fabric in the foreground or the horse-drawn carriage in the far distance. Glackens accurately rendered the topography of the setting—a tumultuous street scene in New York City; his masterful draftsmanship, eye for detail, and insight into the human condition are in full force.

8 Far from the Fresh Air Farm, 1911

Far from the Fresh Air Farm: The crowded city street, with its dangers and temptations, is a pitiful makeshift playground for the children. Crayon heightened with watercolor on paper. 24½ × 16½ inches. Bequest of Ira Glackens. 91.40.152

The drawing known as *Far from the Fresh Air Farm* was published as a full-page illustration in *Collier's* on July 18, 1911, with the caption, "The crowded city street, with its dangers and temptations, is a pitiful makeshift playground for the children." In addition to the threat posed by rearing horses in the middle of the picture, for children the "dangers and temptations" of the street are in this case a direct reference to an article that appeared in the magazine warning of "the dangers of adulterated candy, a great concern in the years leading up to the enactment of pure food and drug laws. In muckraking fashion, this article is illustrated with photographs of children exposed to 'penny poisons' from 'unscrupulous street venders.'"[25] The title also "makes an ironic reference to turn-of-the-century social welfare programs that provided rest and recuperation for sickly slum dwellers and sponsored rural vacations for inner-city children."[26]

If the subject is indeed the threat represented by unscrupulous street vendors who prey on innocent children and the dangers that children encounter in the streets, then it is odd that Glackens relegated the vignettes that illustrate those perils to minor locations within the composition. Indeed, the girls who could be sickened by "penny poison" candy can barely be seen in the shadows beneath the awning on the left, faintly inscribed "CANDY & CIGARS." They are virtually lost in a crowd of passersby, and the children walking across the street, about to be struck by a horse-drawn carriage, are so small and rendered in such pale tonalities that they are barely visible.

Even though the subject is purportedly the plight of urban lower-class children, given the organization of the composition, it appears that the subject is perhaps instead the women who labor to care for the children, shown toiling in the street to support their families. Moreover, although the women in the foreground are emphasized, "[t]hese massive, babushka-wearing figures with scowling demeanors are rarely mentioned in the stories Glackens illustrated, yet they appear in many of his drawings of ghetto scenes."[27] As in *Curb Exchange [No. 3]* (see pl. 7), here women selling produce are once again placed at the front of the composition. In these images the women are seen in profile or with their backs to the viewer as they lean over their pushcarts or baskets, selling their wares. In addition to the female produce vendors, in both works Glackens shows seemingly downtrodden, anonymous women who shuffle slowly with heads down and in some cases with children in tow. Although the artist never professed any overt sympathy or concern for the plight of the masses, often immigrants, who peopled the bustling streets that he loved to draw, an examination of his compositions and depictions of women suggests that he wanted the viewer to notice them and perhaps ponder their circumstances.

The fact that Glackens wants the viewer to focus on the fruit vendor and her customer is abundantly clear not only because he accorded them a prominent position,

literally at the lower center, but also because they are the most brightly colored elements in the picture. A critic once noted that in Glackens's illustrations, "where color is used, it calls to us all the way across the room."[28] In *Far from the Fresh Air Farm*, it is obvious that Glackens wants us to notice the women in the foreground first. The bright red shawl worn by the customer immediately draws our eye to her and to the transaction taking place, and the fruit vendor, although dressed in neutral gray and brown tones, stands beneath a blue and orange umbrella, which once again draws our attention. The bright blue pigment in the umbrella also colors the skirt of a svelte woman on the left who walks arm in arm with a fashionably dressed upper-class woman—perhaps Glackens used color to make us notice the different social classes represented in the picture.

Glackens's sympathy for the plight of the women who figure so prominently in his drawings of urban neighborhoods might in part have been due to his wife's beliefs and concerns. Edith Dimock Glackens, like her mother and sister, Irene, wife of the art critic Charles FitzGerald, was an ardent feminist, a suffragette, and champion of women's rights. Edith was always a spirited freethinker, and, although she came from a wealthy family in Hartford, Connecticut, she nonetheless boldly studied art in New York City in the years before she married. After Edith passed away, an article in the *Hartford Times* about her family noted that "the Dimocks were a convention-breaking family in an age when conventions were just beginning to grow flexible. The two girls, believing in women's rights as their mother did, went to New York to make careers."[29] For her part, Irene, who had studied medicine for a time, later gave up her pursuit of an acting career to work for suffrage as a secretary to Carrie Chapman Catt. Catt was a famous women's suffrage leader who successfully campaigned for the Nineteenth Amendment to the United States Constitution, which in 1920 gave women the right to vote.

In her zealousness, Edith Glackens encouraged (or compelled?) her husband to attend a parade in support of voting rights for women, knowing that he would be scorned by some for attending. Ira Glackens wrote that after the Armory Show of 1913 "had fired a great blast in favor of freedom and a new life, later that same year there came another manifestation for freedom. A great suffrage parade marched down Fifth Avenue, witnessed by enormous crowds. All the Glackenses were ardent suffragists, Edith and William marched in the parade, as did E.'s sister Irene… the women marched in white tailored suits with skirts to the ground and they carried banners in the suffrage colors, purple and gold.… When the men marched briskly by … there were mingled boos and cheers (for their bravery) which could be heard for blocks as they approached. W.G. was among those who got the boos and cheers."[30]

9 Christmas Shoppers, Madison Square, 1912

Crayon and watercolor on paper. 17¼ × 31 inches. Bequest of Ira Glackens. 91.40.106

The drawing now known as *Christmas Shoppers, Madison Square* was published on December 13, 1912, as a two-page illustration in *Collier's Weekly* with the title *The Day before Christmas on Madison Square*.

    Like Glackens's two other famous illustrations of urban views (see pls. 7, 8), *Christmas Shoppers, Madison Square* is now acclaimed as an independent work of art, a beautifully crafted drawing filled with abundant period detail that chronicles the bustling activity at an intersection in New York City that is still heralded as a prime shopping

locale. Today the intersection where Fifth Avenue crosses Broadway at Twenty-Third Street, just west of Madison Square Park, is the center of the Flatiron District, so named because the famed Flatiron Building, completed in 1902, is situated just behind where the artist stood in order to capture this view.

Now as then, the shoppers who flock to the neighborhood are an upscale lot drawn to the markets and shops that occupy almost the entire ground floor of the city block where the Garfield National Bank, shown in Glackens's view at left, was located in 1912. Visitors to the area will recognize the clock on the sidewalk just behind the horse and buggy on the left side of Fifth Avenue. The clock still stands there today, keeping accurate time as it has since it was set in place in 1909. The plaque on the clock reads, "This 1909 Iconic Street Clock Was Designated a New York City Landmark in 1981" and "Tiffany and Company Restored the Clock as a Gift to the Historic Flatiron District."

Unlike the other bustling street scenes, there are no large figures in the foreground singled out for our immediate attention; rather, Glackens presents a friezelike tableau of people scampering left and right and back and forth in the street and on the sidewalk, seen from an elevated perspective.[31] In the immediate foreground he drew them with precise detail, including a pickpocket reaching into the purse of an unsuspecting woman waiting to cross the street—one of the many vignettes that fill every inch of space within the drawing.

Given the scale and coloration he accorded them, the varied modes of transportation—bright green buses and trolleys, a yellow car, and a red wagon—seem to have been the artist's primary focus. The one figure who does, however, stand out in the teeming throng—dressed in bright red and placed at the center of the composition so that he cannot be missed—is a man dressed in a Santa Claus suit. In the same way that Glackens used bright red pigment to draw our attention to the shawl worn by a lower-class woman in the foreground of *Far from the Fresh Air Farm*, in *Christmas Shoppers, Madison Square* the same red highlights the Santa Claus figure, shown ringing a bell next to a kettle with a partially legible sign that reads "X MASS" and "POOR." As if once again to ask that the viewer consider the plight of the less fortunate, Glackens shows a fashionably dressed upper-class woman stopping to make a donation.

10 Cape Cod Pier, 1908

Oil on canvas. 26 × 32 inches. Gift of an anonymous donor. 85.74

Cape Cod Pier is a crucial work that represents a major turning point in Glackens's evolving style, as he turned away from the dark, muted earth-toned palette of Henri and moved into the sun-drenched colorism of the Impressionists. Glackens visited Cape Cod in 1908; "it was during this period that, perhaps inspired by the presence of and conversations with [Maurice] Prendergast, who visited at some point during the season, Glackens began to transform his method of painting...likely stimulated by the bright and colorful scenery of the beaches on the Cape."[32]

While the stylistic shift can certainly be accounted for by examining influences from the artists whose works Glackens had emulated, it is also possible, indeed probable, that the exuberance of his new palette reflected the pleasure he felt in the lovely

HOTEL NOBSCUSSET,   DENNIS, CAPE COD, MASS.

Fig. 9 Hotel Nobscussett. Postcard, c. 1910–1915. Photograph courtesy of the Postcard Collection, Dennis Historical Society, Dennis, Massachusetts

settings he discovered—the places where he happily spent time with his family and friends that became subjects for his art. He was not simply an artist passively recording a scene he observed—he was a participant, and in the new, more colorful paintings "his genius for transforming his inner joyousness to canvas," was clearly in evidence.[33]

Cape Cod Pier was painted on the grounds of the Nobscussett Hotel in the beach town of Dennis, Massachusetts (fig. 9). Built in 1872 it sat "high on the bluff overlooking Cape Cod Bay, one of the most luxurious resorts on Cape Cod until it closed in 1929 during the great Depression...Along the bluff near the water's edge at the Nobscussett Hotel stood a large bath house pavilion, including a covered balcony on the top...to take in sea views. There was also a pier for guest use that extended out several hundred feet into the bay."[34] The bath house pavilion appears on the right in *Cape Cod Pier*. Since the pier and bathhouse depicted in the painting (figs. 10–12) had been added to the grand hotel in 1888 "for guest use," the Glackens family may have stayed there before moving into the house in Dennis that they had rented for the summer. Glackens did many sketches of the pier and bathhouse, several showing the covered balcony above, where guests relaxed in hammocks as they enjoyed cool breezes and views of the sea (figs. 13, 14).

In formulating his new style, Glackens was clearly inspired by the works of the Impressionists, seen when he traveled to Paris as a young artist in 1896 and more recently on his delayed honeymoon ten years later, but he was also perhaps more

THE PATH TO THE BATH HOUSES AND BEACH, HOTEL NOBSCUSSET,   DENNIS, MASS.

Fig. 10 Bathhouse pavilion. Postcard, by H. A. Dickerman & Son, c. 1910–1915. Florrie Hall Collection, Dennis Historical Society

Fig. 11 Nobscussett beach and pier. Photograph, c. 1915. Jean Twiss Collection, Dennis Historical Society. Clara E. (Nichols) Twiss worked as a maid at the hotel. Photograph courtesy of the Dennis Historical Society, Dennis, Massachusetts

Fig. 12 View of Nobscussett Beach in Dennis looking toward the bluff where the bathhouse pavilion once stood and the location of the pier's foundation. Photograph, by the author, August 2012

Fig. 13 Preparatory drawing for the Nobscussett bathhouse pavilion and beach in "W. Glackens Cape Cod" (sketchbook), 1908. Graphite on paper. 9 × 5½ inches. Gift of the Sansom Foundation. 94.132

Fig. 14 Preparatory drawing for Nobscussett pier in "W. Glackens Cape Cod" (sketchbook), 1908. Graphite on paper. 9 × 5½ inches. Gift of the Sansom Foundation. 94.132

directly influenced by the efforts of his American counterparts. Most notably, his new, more coloristic, and "ruggedly textured Impressionist technique" was prompted by the intense colors of Maurice Prendergast's work, the thick impasto Marsden Hartley had employed in his Maine landscapes, and the brushwork of Ernest Lawson.[35] After studying the paintings of his peers, Glackens proceeded to create a wholly original luminous picture with a lush surface of thickly layered pigment that defines simplified shapes with jarring colors. The result is an image that scintillates, as if emanating from the warmth of the beach on a hot, sunny day while clearly expressing the artist's glee in finding himself there to enjoy it.

Another comparable work dating from this seminal period, in which the dark tones and loose, slapdash technique of his early style were definitively abandoned under the example of modernist tendencies, is *Race Track* (fig. 15) purchased by Glackens's close friend Dr. Albert Barnes and now considered the centerpiece of the Barnes Foundation's famed collection of modern American art, a status comparable to that of *Cape Cod Pier* at the Museum of Art | Fort Lauderdale.[36]

The favorable assessment of the shift in style that works like *Race Track* and *Cape Cod Pier* represent was summed up by a critic reviewing an exhibition at the National

Fig. 15 *Race Track*, 1908–1909. Oil on canvas. 26⅛ × 32¼ inches. Image © The Barnes Foundation. BF 138

Arts Club in 1910. He described Glackens's "brand new manner," noting, "one can fairly wallow in reds and greens in W Glackens' 'Race Track.' If Mr. Glackens thus sees his nature, he must enjoy life far more than the ordinarily equipped human, for there is a riot of tone in his vision." The same critic also commented on Glackens' "aggressively insistent" color.[37]

Also, on the occasion of an exhibition at the Folsom Gallery in March 1913, concurrent with the Armory Show, a critic wrote about Glackens new style: "With a sense of wonderful color palpitating about us, we should like to retrace our steps to the Folsom Gallery again and to stay indefinitely … with the collection of paintings by William Glackens. A more complete realization of all that color can accomplish on canvas has never been presented, we think, in one private exhibition in New York, and presented with a variety that is so infinite that it is as though Nature had shared with Mr. Glackens the splendor of her most prodigal moods."[38]

The preparatory sketches Glackens drew as he worked out the final composition for *Cape Cod Pier* reveal the artist's creative process. The drawings all were done from a vantage point looking back at the beach and dunes from the end of the pier, but in one (fig. 16), which clearly shows the Nobscusett Hotel bathhouse on the bluffs overlooking the water, no figures are present, and in another (fig. 17), a man leans on the pier railing on the right, standing comfortably, relaxing with his legs crossed, smoking either a pipe or a cigarette. He is sketched in more darkly than the women walking ahead, and his clothes have more detail so Glackens must have considered including

Fig. 16 Preparatory drawing of Nobscussett pier for *Cape Cod Pier* (85.74) in "W. Glackens Cape Cod" (sketchbook), 1908. Graphite on paper. 9 × 5½ inches. Gift of the Sansom Foundation. 94.132

Fig. 17 Preparatory drawing of Nobscussett pier for *Cape Cod Pier* (85.74) in "W. Glackens Cape Cod" sketchbook, 1908. Graphite on paper. 9 × 5½ inches. Gift of the Sansom Foundation. 94.132

him in the painting. He may have been omitted from the final composition so as not to impede the viewer's appreciation of the sweeping space that leads down the pier, up and over the dunes, to the brilliant blue sky in the distance.

The locale in *Cape Cod Pier* is clearly one that Glackens embraced, and since he identified with the figures taking a leisurely stroll on the pier or relaxing at the water's edge, he shared that experience with the viewer. The composition opens out toward us as we view the expansive pier from the vantage point of the women strolling in front of us—we vicariously walk behind them, taking in the vista that they and the artist enjoyed.

11 Wickford Low Tide, 1909

Oil on canvas. 25 × 30 inches. Gift of the Sansom Foundation. 94.69

This painting dates from the summer of 1909, when the Glackens family vacationed in Wickford, Rhode Island, near Narragansett Bay. Like *Cape Cod Pier* and *Race Track* (see pl. 10 and fig. 15), radical works completed the year before, *Wickford Low Tide* is another example of the new direction Glackens was pursuing as he experimented with dazzling color effects and richly encrusted surfaces. The simple composition of *Wickford Low Tide*—composed primarily of horizontal bands that describe a rocky beach, shallow pools of water, sand bars, open water, and then distant sky—afforded the artist the opportunity to experiment with the tactile and chromatic qualities of pigment as he layered thick daubs of paint in the foreground beneath thinner crosshatched strokes at the top of the canvas.

Even though Glackens had traveled to Wickford, a seaside locale, with his family, he included no figures shown enjoying the view. Unlike most of the other beach scenes he painted throughout his life, people are oddly absent from the scene. This is in contrast to an early sketch, in which a small figure of a clam digger or a wading bather appeared in the water close to the horizon line (fig. 18). The elimination of the figure, which further simplified the final composition, suggests that the work may have been an exercise, an exploration into formal possibilities. As Glackens was finding his way with his new style, perhaps his innate exuberance was now directed toward his pigments and the newfound qualities of color and surface that they afforded him, rather than toward a representation of the people who so often had filled his pictures in the past. And while the emphasis may be on the formal traits of texture and color, the foreground space still opens out to the viewer: we can vicariously walk along the rocky shore and see the rocks and water glinting in the sun.

The manner in which Glackens's new post-Ashcan style was evolving was described by a critic assessing another beach scene, *The Bathing Hour, Chester, Nova Scotia* (Barnes Foundation, Philadelphia) painted the year after *Wickford Low Tide*. Both works possess pronounced tactile qualities with vibrant colors thickly applied with vigorous brushstrokes in the foreground. "His color grows more harmonious, though it often shocks by its brilliant dissonances.... Beaches of inland seas, the waters of which are vivid blues; skies as hard blue as Italy's, white cloud boulders that roll lazily across the field of vision ... nothing tempered as would a less sincere artist, but set forth unmodulated and in audacious oppositions, these waters, skies, beaches ... are nevertheless so real, or evoke the illusion of reality, that you experience in their presence what Henry James calls 'emotion of recognition.'"[39]

Fig. 18 Preparatory drawing for *Wickford, Low Tide* (94.69) in "W. Glackens Wickford, Color List" (sketchbook), 1909. Charcoal on paper. 8½ × 5¾ inches. Gift of the Sansom Foundation. 94.101

12 Twenty-Three Fifth Avenue, Interior, c. 1910

Oil on canvas. 19½ × 24 inches. Bequest of Ira Glackens. 91.40.135

The Museum of Art | Fort Lauderdale collection is significant because of the master-works by Glackens that it contains, but also, from the standpoint of understanding and illuminating the artist's working habits, it holds invaluable examples of smaller works painted as studies for larger compositions. As such, they reveal Glackens's creative process and also stand alone as independent works with abundant aesthetic merit. One example is *Twenty-Three Fifth Avenue, Interior*, of about 1910, certainly painted as a study of the empty room that the artist would soon paint again, occupied by family and friends in his widely acclaimed and much-admired *Family Group* (fig. 19). *Twenty-Three Fifth Avenue, Interior*, a cozy domestic view, accurately records the appearance of the living room in the apartment that the Glackenses rented at the time, while displaying the loose brushwork and bold color that were soon to become hallmarks of his mature style.

Although it may have been painted as a study for the larger figurative composition, *Twenty-Three Fifth Avenue, Interior* is nonetheless a handsome work in which Glackens faithfully conveys the warm, intimate ambience of his comfortable home, largely through his use of light. The sun casts long, late afternoon shadows, visible outside the open door on an iron balcony, and a sliver of light faintly illuminates an otherwise darkened room. The foreground is left open, as if to welcome the viewer into the room, to offer us a seat in his elegant home.

Fig. 19
Family Group, 1910–1911.
Oil on canvas. 71¹⁵⁄₁₆ × 84 inches. Image courtesy of the National Gallery of Art, Washington; Gift of Mr. and Mrs. Ira Glackens 1971.12.1

Fig. 20 *Twenty-Three Fifth
Avenue, Interior*, detail
showing chair

Inspired by Impressionist painting techniques, Glackens used thick, vigorous brush-strokes to suggest the varied textures found in the furnishings of the room: elaborate, swift, curving strokes describe the pattern on the wing chair (fig. 20) and the inlaid table, and crosshatched strokes describe the pattern in the rugs. Glackens's palette, with its rich, deep hues, can be seen as harking back to his earlier canvases, but in this case the darker colors accurately describe the dark furnishings in a darkened room. And though dark in value, many vibrant notes appear, most notably in the reds, which range from vermilion to deep rose red to burgundy.

Glackens made many sketchbook studies of the room and its furnishings with and without family members present; they attest to his keen eye for detail and nuance in pose and gesture (figs. 21–23). *Twenty-Three Fifth Avenue, Interior* hangs at the Museum of Art | Fort Lauderdale in a room that is a re-creation of the living room shown in the picture. The painting and the room are filled with the furniture, paintings, and decorative objects that belonged to the Glackens family—treasured possessions that the artist proudly displayed in his home and lovingly depicted in his art.

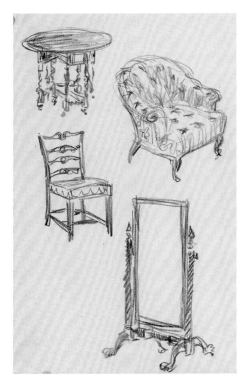

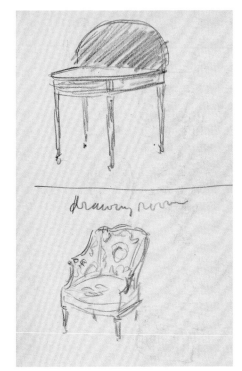

Figs. 21–23 Three preparatory drawings for *Twenty-Three Fifth Avenue, Interior* (91.40.135) in "W. Glackens NY, Skating in Park" (sketchbook), not dated. Charcoal and graphite on paper. 8 × 5½ inches. Gift of the Sansom Foundation. 94.100

13 Sledding in Central Park, 1912

Oil on canvas. 23 × 31½ inches. Bequest of Ira Glackens. 91.40.150

Writing in 1931, when Glackens was showing new work at the Kraushaar Gallery in New York, the critic Mary Fanton Roberts eloquently described his "genius" as a painter, referencing a sledding scene in Central Park. She described him as "essentially a great colorist and an artist with a witty appreciation of life. That is why one has such a sense of living quality in all he paints … and what a quality of vivid joy pervades his painting of a group of little children running through Central Park over frosted ground, with their bright-colored sleds."[40]

The "vivid joy" found in *Sledding in Central Park* is shared by the artist's son Ira, a five-year-old seen from behind dressed in a Scottish outfit with his sled in tow. New York City's Central Park was a favored locale for Glackens and his fellow Ashcan painters. With Robert Henri, he "and their circle made something of a specialty of views of Central Park, a site they also visited for skating and relaxation," and although he simply chose a subject that was personally meaningful to him, "of all the urban landscapes that

Glackens painted during the century's first decade, none received more public exposure than his Central Park views."[41] The pictures were surely popular for the "sense of living quality" that pervades them.

The painting is an example of one of Glackens's many scenes of people enjoying outdoor activities during different seasons of the year. New York City parks were a frequent subject for Glackens, most notably Washington Square Park, located near his studio in Greenwich Village, and here Central Park—the vast expanse of property designed as a backyard for recreation and renewal for millions of urban apartment dwellers.

A version of a similar view from seven years earlier, *Central Park, Winter* (fig. 24), which features Glackens's darker palette, displays the prominent silhouette of an adult in the foreground, a woman seemingly looming in the shadows as she protectively watches her child pulling a sled in the foreground. In *Sledding in Central Park*, the space is more expansive, and the dark shadows of the earlier work have been replaced by a panoramic view of a sunny park with light flickering everywhere off the surface of the snow. The coloristic experiments of the 1907–1909 period have now been fully absorbed into Glackens's mature style, inspired by Impressionism, and now characterized by boldness in both brushstroke and color.

There is also a change in tone in the later work, in which, rather than giving the protective, watchful adult a dominant presence in the foreground, a comparable figure, also leaning against a tree, is diminished in size and placed in the distant middle ground on the left. She still performs her watchful duties, looking out over the children frolicking in the snow, but by placing her in the distance Glackens consciously gave the open foreground over to the numerous children enjoying the fun-filled abandon of sledding. And as if their joyfulness were not already made clear by their small bodies in motion sliding in the snow or climbing back up to the crest of the hill for another ride down,

Fig. 24
Central Park, Winter, c. 1905
Oil on canvas. 25 × 30 inches
The Metropolitan Museum
of Art, George A. Hearn
Fund, 1921 (21.164). Image ©
The Metropolitan Museum
of Art

Glackens's colors express their glee, especially the sharp bright red used on the hat and coat of the girl seated on her sled (fig. 25). For pictorial unity and to further express the gaiety of the scene, Glackens used the same bright red to color the sled in the middle of the picture, and, adding to the dynamism of the colors, the brushwork is energetic, with vigorous, curved strokes that fly off on diagonals to suggest the texture created by the movement of the sleds across the snow.

Here in the park on a sunny winter day, the artist shared his experience as a parent enjoying playful time with his young son and the joy of an artist capable of capturing and conveying that happy experience to those who view the picture.

Fig. 25
Sledding in Central Park, detail showing girl in red sledding

14 Children Rollerskating, after 1913

Oil on canvas. 18 × 24 inches. Gift of the Sansom Foundation. 92.37

Like *Central Park Sledding* (see pl. 13), this picture presents children at play, but the drama that appears to unfold in the foreground is an ambiguous one. The two skaters in blue and green reach out to the skater in orange, who is just beyond their reach, and while they could be chasing her as she flees, they could also be lunging toward her protectively to catch her if she loses her footing on the curved path. No matter what the specific narrative might be, the overall feeling of the work is lyrical, largely due to the prevalence of decorative patterns and cheerful, vibrant colors.[42] The work reflects a joie de vivre that could have been inspired by Henri Matisse, the Fauve master with whom Glackens shared numerous stylistic affinities.

A virtually identical watercolor study for this oil painting was subtitled *A Decoration*, and that is the clue to the relationship of *Children Rollerskating* to an unusual group of works that Glackens painted in the winter of 1914–1915. He exhibited them the following spring at the Montross Gallery in New York City, "in a group show of modern American art, some of which was specifically designed for decoration."[43] Another work included in that exhibition from a group entitled the "Hindu" paintings was *Buddha and the Maidens* (fig. 26), and it, too, was subtitled *A Decoration.* The figures of the maidens in the latter picture and the children in *Children Roller-skating* all have elongated, sinuous bodies with outstretched arms, and they occupy landscapes made of flattened, curvilinear shapes and colorful, decorative patterns. The stylistical similarities in these two experimental works are abundantly clear, and the fact that the artist designated them both *Decoration* further confirms that he thought they were related. Ira Glackens thought so, too; he asserted that *Buddha and the Maidens* was one in "an experimental series, done as decoration for a lampshade for Edith."[44] Another work in the series, simply titled *Decoration*, is owned by the Barnes Foundation.

Glackens was fascinated with roller-skating as a subject, and he would explore it again in a work with the same title (fig. 27). In that work depicting children on roller skates in Washington Square Park, he presents the subject in a more traditional style—though the two primary skaters move toward us stiffly and cautiously, they nonetheless share the more innocent playful, spirit found in works like *Sledding in Central Park.*

Fig. 26 *Buddha and the Maidens (Decorative Panel)*, c. 1914–1916. Oil on canvas. 48 × 30 inches. Gift of the Sansom Foundation. 94.5

Fig. 27 *Children Rollerskating*, c. 1912–1914. Oil on canvas. 23⅞ × 18 inches. Brooklyn Museum, Bequest of Laura L. Barnes. 67.24.1

15 Mother with a Baby, Washington Square Park, 1914

Oil on canvas. 14¼ × 17½ inches. Bequest of Ira Glackens. 91.40.137

Glackens painted many scenes of Washington Square Park, often recording what he observed from his third-floor studio window that overlooked it from the south. From this perch, Glackens could see the myriad activities that took place in the park year round. *Mother with a Baby* is set in the warmer months, but the bright green grass was covered with snow and mud in earlier Washington Square views such as *The Green Car* (fig. 28) from 1910.

Here the mother balancing her infant in her arms is larger than the figures in the earlier compositions and placed in the foreground closer to the viewer. She seems to strain to hold on to her squirming child as the baby's head turns toward the activity taking place in the middle ground behind them. Again the foreground is open to us,

Fig. 28 *The Green Car*, 1910. Oil on canvas. 24 × 32 inches. The Metropolitan Museum of Art, Arthur Hoppock Hearn Fund, 1937 (37.73). Image © The Metropolitan Museum of Art

so that we can enter the path and join this woman dressed in simple garb, perhaps a resident of the lower-class Italian neighborhood that bordered the park on the south. Glackens may have been acknowledging his neighbors when he chose to include in this park view the statue of Giuseppe Garibaldi that had been given to the city of New York by the Italian American community in 1888.

As a resident of New York City, Glackens was everywhere witness to its melting-pot quality, and he freely recorded the varied ethnic groups and social classes he found intermingled in public settings. Modes of public transportation are the subject of earlier Washington Square Park paintings, and in *Mother with a Baby* he included a fancy and no doubt expensive bright red automobile, and in other park views Glackens portrayed members of the upper classes who resided above the park on Fifth Avenue, such as the fashionably dressed woman hailing the streetcar in *The Green Car*. He also acknowledged the efforts of municipal workers who maintained the park as an oasis for all to enjoy: a street sweeper in a clean white uniform is seen at work behind the mother and child here, and others like him are the subject of *Street Cleaners, Washington Square* (fig. 29).

Compared with the Washington Square views completed four years earlier, *Mother with a Baby* displays looser and more vigorous brushwork, with distinctive patches

Fig. 29 *Street Cleaners, Washington Square*, c. 1910. Oil on canvas. 25¼ × 30 inches. Image © The Barnes Foundation. BF2035

of white impasto, and the color contrasts are more jarring, perhaps because the scene is illuminated by bright sun. The influence of recent avant-garde French painting can clearly be seen in the blue shadows cast by the red trees and in the mother's bold turquoise skirt, set against emerald green grass. She passes by a vermilion curb, and that color appears again on the car, the trunk of the tree in the foreground, and on the town house facades in the distance, where it is once again set off against emerald green. While stylistically displaying modernist concerns, the picture can also be seen as another example of Glackens's innate joie de vivre as he celebrated the cheery bustle of the city as it played out before him.

16 Artist's Daughter in Chinese Costume, 1918

Oil on canvas. 48 × 30 inches. Gift of the Sansom Foundation. 92.28

This painting, and other figure studies of the period, can be seen as examples of

> part of a general shift in orientation away from the public sphere and toward the private
> studio and personal spaces of his home.... Glackens's continued exploration of vibrant color
> relationships coincided with his increased interest in more mundane and subdued subject
> matter. As he turned from painting multifigural scenes of kinetic movement to static subjects
> that include portrait sitters, nude models, and still life objects, however, the sense of action
> and movement characteristic of his outdoor scenes migrated from animated pictorial content
> to his own vigorous brushwork which emphasizes the artist's activity, not as recorder of urban
> life or beach scenes, but as a painter of canvases.[45]

The Glackens children or their parents seem to have had a penchant for exotic garb.
Ira appeared in *Sledding in Central Park*, six years earlier, in a Scottish outfit, complete
with kilt, to go sledding on a snowy day, and here Lenna looks sweet and poised as she
poses gracefully in a large, billowing Chinese costume. *Artist's Daughter in Chinese Costume* is an especially charming work and one of the most popular and widely exhibited
paintings that Glackens created.

The picture combines a favored subject—a beloved family member—with the artist's elegant, painterly style at its best, displaying feathered brushwork inspired by Pierre-
Auguste Renoir. Glackens's natural affinity for rich, glowing color and resplendent

decorative patterns is everywhere in evidence, and the painting's cheerful brightness can be seen as expressing the happy personality of Lenna as well as her father's affection for her. The personal quality of the work extends to the frame, which Glackens hand-carved. For several years he had been friends with the Prendergast brothers, Maurice and Charles, fellow artists who owned a successful framing business in Boston and later in New York City. Glackens was no doubt inspired by their efforts—perhaps after Charles had made frames for some of his canvases.

Unlike his earlier paintings in which pigments varied from lightly brushed, thin oil washes to more thickly painted areas of impasto, the painted surface in *Artist's Daughter in Chinese Costume* is evenly painted throughout, with forms defined by long, soft, feathered strokes. The dominant red colors range from deep corals and roses to almost burgundy hues—all standing in sharp contrast to the cool blues of the Chinese costume and the patch of deep green between the drapes. This riot of warm and cool colors and lively decorative patterns is an elegant foil for the head of young Lenna—her face painted delicately in a soft, creamy white with a hint of pink to suggest her lightly flushed cheeks, and blue eyes that match the ribbon that ties back her hair.

In addition to the exquisite formal traits—the rich colors and lush surface that distinguish the work—its most endearing quality is surely the winsome expression that Glackens so masterfully captured on his daughter's face. With her head turned slightly to the side, her hand resting gracefully on the chair, and her dreamy gaze, she is the picture of a sweet and contented child—a photograph showing her smiling widely while wearing the costume confirms the cheery disposition that her father portrayed (fig. 30).

17 House in Conway, 1920

Oil on canvas. 30 × 25 inches. Gift of the Sansom Foundation. 91.40.18

In his memoir, *William Glackens and the Eight*, Ira Glackens described the rustic "pioneer existence" the family enjoyed during the years they spent summering in Conway, New Hampshire, beginning in 1920, noting that it was "a puzzle" that his mother, who had been "brought up in comfort, seemed happy and contented without any plumbing." Nonetheless, despite the absence of electricity or running water, the house "proved so satisfactory that five summers were spent there.... Life was simple and neighbors not too near. The country was heavily wooded and very hilly, and there were fine walks as well as some mountain climbing.... In spite of the pioneer existence in Conway, E. did not hesitate to invite friends to visit and share the primitive life."[46]

Ira explained that although Conway lies in the foothills of the White Mountains, his father, an avid fisherman, "did not care much to paint mountains, as they afford no foregrounds, but the small-mouthed black bass in Conway Lake … were then prodigious.... If the painting in Conway was not very good, the fishing was." With that said,

when Glackens tore himself away from fishing with a rod Robert Henri had given him, making new fishing rods, or practicing casting in a pond on the property, he "produced a few landscapes and some flower pieces and still lifes when the need to paint grew too great and the out-of-doors was too green and buggy; but on the whole Conway seems not to have provided many paintable places." "Only when the autumn colors began and the landscape grew less green were the paints usually brought out."[47]

Even if he lamented the scarcity of "paintable places," Glackens nonetheless produced two luminous depictions of the rustic house where the family enjoyed leisure time away from the heat of the city, and they both represent his mature Impressionist landscape style at its best. *House in Conway*, with its sumptuous, glowing colors and lively brushwork, clearly expresses the joyfulness Glackens felt while spending time in a peaceful, pastoral setting with his loved ones close at hand.

In *House in Conway* Glackens's passion for the expressive possibilities of vivid contrasting colors is everywhere in evidence—most notably in the contrast between the rich jewel greens of the trees and shrubs and the purple and fuchsia pink tree seen in silhouette next to the bright orange house, with its emerald green shutters and dormer windows painted in blue-green and pink hues.

In addition to the vibrant colors, the variety of energetic brushstrokes demonstrates the artist's glee; filled with verve, they range from soft, long strokes on the rolling lawn and the trees, rustling in the summer breeze, to the shorter dashed strokes that describe flickering sunlight falling on shrubs and flowers. Overall, Glackens created shimmering contrasts between the warm oranges of the house and the cool purples, greens, and dark blues of the trees and shrubs that shade it, with the thickest dabs of paint reserved for the sharp pink and white that color the flowers growing near the door.

18 Breakfast Porch, 1925

Oil on canvas. 30 × 25 inches. Gift of the Sansom Foundation. 92.30

Breakfast Porch was painted in France in the summer of 1925, on the first European excursion for the Glackens family, one that began an extended stay abroad that lasted through 1931.[48] In his memoir, Ira Glackens described the summer house where they settled in Samois-sur-Seine, a town where Glackens's artist friend Leon Kroll had a home. The Glackenses' house was called "the Maison Daboncourt and had been built in the late seventeenth century; in the rear was a fine walled garden containing an *orangerie*."[49]

Since it was Edith's habit to arrange bowls of fruit and vases of flowers to decorate their home, we can assume that it was she who chose the bouquet of yellow, orange, and white zinnias and cosmos that fills the large basket that dominates the lower half of the composition. Whereas the weave of the basket and petals of the flowers are painted lavishly, with careful attention to detail—especially the curling petals of the white cosmos—the rest of the composition, the oddly glum or sleepy figures and the cramped space they occupy, is painted with the long, blurry, feathered strokes that were characteristic of Glackens's Renoir-esque style at the time.

Breakfast Porch is an enigmatic work, which, because of the bright colors and decorative flowers, at first seems to convey a cheerful, lighthearted mood. However, incongruities emerge on closer study, and the painting becomes perplexing, with the figures appearing as a "strangely solemn and hermetic assembly."[50]

The porch where the Glackenses ate breakfast in their seventeenth-century house in Samois-sur-Seine may have been as small and cramped as the room shown here, but, if so, it was surely an uncomfortable place to dine. The fact that Edith and her children are clustered so snugly around the table might account for their dour expressions, or perhaps, again, they were all still sleepy as they gathered for their morning meal. Be that as it may, the bold, vibrant, cheerful colors in the picture are at odds with the demeanor of the figures.

In the past, when Glackens depicted his family, for example, *The Artist's Wife and Son*, 1911 (Snite Museum of Art, University of Notre Dame, Notre Dame, Ind.), he had used compressed space—placing the figures in a room with densely packed furniture—

Fig. 31 *Portrait of Edith*, c. 1925.
Pastel on paper. 10 × 7¼ inches.
Bequest of Ira Glackens. 91.40.42

to suggest familial bonding. In that earlier picture, Edith's gesture as she lovingly wraps her arms around her son, emphatically encircling him, and the tight space they occupy enhance the sentiment expressed. In *Breakfast Porch*, however, although the mother and children share a close physical space, they are aloof, emotionally distant from one another.

If their moods may be attributed to morning drowsiness, the children, though not shown interacting, are at least eating their meal—Lenna raises a spoon to her mouth, and Ira, whose eyes appear to be completely closed, nonetheless lifts a cup. Edith, by contrast, is engaged with neither a meal nor her children. Instead, with downcast eyes and her hand held to her cheek, she turns to the side and appears to be psychologically and emotionally absent.

Adding to Edith's gloomy persona is the black shadow looming behind her head, an odd compositional element in Glackens's work at the time. A clue to Edith's demeanor might be found in a dark pastel study (fig. 31). In this work, drawn with black crayon and sepia and brown chalk, Glackens used the same thick, coal black color as appears behind his wife's head in the painting. In the drawing, the use of black logically suggests a cast shadow, but, with downcast eyes and hand held to her face, Edith can also be seen as expressing sadness or dismay. With that said, depicting Edith as pensive, withdrawn, docile, or glum, especially in a work in which she is shown with her children, is peculiar, because, by all accounts, she was known to be a feisty, vivacious, and free-spirited woman who gleefully embraced life as fully as her husband did. His portrayal of her in *Breakfast Porch*, therefore, is out of character with the woman she was purported to be.

19 Along the Marne, after 1925

Oil on board. 12½ × 15½ inches. Bequest of Ira Glackens. 91.40.107

Both *House in Conway* (see pl. 17) and *Along the Marne* are fond representations of locales where Glackens spent vacation time with his family, and both display his mature Renoir-esque landscape style at its best, with soft, feathered brushstrokes used to apply colors in rich, jewel tones. After having spent five years summering in Conway, New Hampshire, from 1920 to 1924, the Glackens family began an extended seven-year stay in Europe, passing the summer of 1925 in Samois-sur-Seine. It was during this European sojourn that both *Breakfast Porch* (see pl. 18) and *Along the Marne* were painted, the first time that Glackens and his wife had gone back to France since their honeymoon in 1906, now returning with their family in tow.

Along the Marne, one of Glackens's most overtly romantic images, can perhaps be seen as expressing the artist's nostalgia for the honeymoon trip, while at the same time celebrating the closeness they still shared as they returned with their two children.

Fig. 32 *Beach at Dieppe*, 1906. Oil on canvas. 24 × 32 inches. Image © The Barnes Foundation. BF562

When they first visited the area in 1906, the couple had spent a few days in Dieppe, and in *Beach at Dieppe* (fig. 32), Glackens included himself and his new bride standing side by side on the right side of the painting with their backs to the viewer as they look out at the crowd gathered by the water's edge.[51] The couple that appears alone on the sunny path at the center of *Along the Marne* could once again be Glackens and his wife, sharing a romantic, nostalgic moment later in life.

The romantic content of *Along the Marne* is something of an anomaly in Glackens's oeuvre because, according to his son, the artist was known to be shy by nature and uncomfortable expressing his feelings. "The reason these two had let so much time slip by without mutually discovering their feelings lay mostly in W.G.'s reticent nature; he was unable to say what he thought ... he referred in a letter to 'my miserable shyness.' But E. could not break down his reserve. He invariably called her 'Miss Dimock' until in despair she warned 'if you call me that again, I will kiss you in front of everyone.' This threat had the desired effect."[52]

An expression of Glackens's affection for Edith can be found in a letter and drawing he sent to her in the summer of 1903; in the drawing the fashionable straw boater that is later shown tucked under the artist's arm in *Beach at Dieppe* also appears. The love letter to Edith Dimock, his future bride, sent the year before they married, references a boat trip Glackens took alone across the Hudson River from the Palisades in New

Jersey (fig. 33). The inscription, starting on the back and continuing to the front over his drawing, reads,

> I took a ferry from the Palisades and spent an hour being blown about on top of them. I sat in a summer garden on the very edge of the cliff [where] we could see all over the world almost, and drank a great glass of that same beer … we had at Van's that day. I invoked your spirit and we had a fine time all by ourselves. Your hair was blown all about your face, just as it would have been and many a circle within a circle passed between us—it was the next best thing to having you really there.

In the drawing, Glackens shows his straw boater blown away in the wind, with an arrow pointing to it and a caption reading, "the memorable hat."

Glackens shows the couple seated together at a café table overlooking the river with the New York City skyline in the distance. They lean in close toward one another, and, their heads and hands almost touching, Glackens creates a closely shared space that mimics the "circle within a circle" he described; Ira Glackens referred to the drawing as "a sketch of his tête-à-tête with the imaginary Edith."[53] In all three of these sentimental renderings, Glackens used poses and gestures expressively, as he had so often done in his illustrations; the couple huddling close in the 1903 drawing was depicted as the newly-weds standing side by side in 1906 on the beach in Dieppe, and again strolling alone on a secluded path in *Along the Marne* more than twenty years later. The fact that in the later work Glackens placed the affectionate couple at the center of the composition, as he had in his earlier drawing, may indicate that his intent was to demonstrate more overtly the romantic content of the work.

Fig. 33 *Love Letter to Edith Dimock*, c. 1903. Ink and wash on paper. 9½ × 7½ inches. Gift of the Sansom Foundation. 92.133

20 Bowlers, La Ciotat, 1930

Oil on canvas. 25 × 30 inches. Gift of the Sansom Foundation. 92.31

This picture was painted when the family was summering at the Villa des Cytharis in La Ciotat, a town in the South of France. Ira Glackens described the villa as "having an enormous flagstoned terrace, eighty feet long, stretching across the front of it and looking out over the tops of olive trees to the bay of La Ciotat." In recollecting the family's time there, he wrote, "with its harbor full of fishing boats, the festivities on Bastille Day … the evenings now and then at the little casino near the beach, the daily dip in the Mediterranean—all of these diversions combined to make the summer pass too rapidly … in spite of which this was a fine, productive summer for W.G."[54]

Just as he had recorded in great detail the local activities that unfolded around him first as an artist-reporter and then as an artist in New York City, so too while vacationing in southern France, Glackens faithfully recorded in his art the local flavor and customs he found so endearing. During his stay,

> the lives of the local *azuréens* cast their spell on Glackens. At La Ciotat, near Marseille, he painted several versions of local men playing *boules*, a traditional Mediterranean game…. With a palette and feathery paint handling borrowed from Renoir, Glackens creates a picture of timeless pastoral entertainment. Four men, all sporting the kind of nautical headgear that is typical of the region, watch a fifth man pitch the small metal ball; he leans just slightly forward from the waist, with arm extended, in the approved manner. The game transpires in a grove of five pine trees, as afternoon light illuminates the scene, causing the pines to cast long shadows. A sixth tree, at the extreme right edge of the painting, echoes the leftward tilt of the bowler (several trees here lean left, blown that way by the winds from the sea)….
>   Glackens's picture is a synthesis of a way of life.[55]

Inspired by the light of southern France, this image of bowlers engaged in casual recreation captures the mood of a lazy summer afternoon. The realistic rendering of the long shadows and the architecture is the only concession that Glackens made to naturalistic representation, and the rest of this work, with its simplified forms and exaggerated colors, reflects a much more modernist sensibility. Indeed, the composition is defined by repeated curvilinear forms—including those of the treetops and distant mountains, juxtaposed against the angular, geometric shapes of the building. The composition can be seen as a foray into modernist simplification and abstraction, enhanced by long strokes of vibrant color—golden ocher grass, a coral roof, blue and purple shadows, vivid green and yellow foliage, and turquoise water.

Bowlers, La Ciotat can also been seen as harking back to more decorative works such as *Children Rollerskating* (see pl. 14), in which Glackens had experimented with sinuous, elongated forms. They appear in the figures' limbs and the landscape in the earlier work, as they do here, most notably in the swerving tree trunks. The overall decorative quality of the work may also reflect the influence of Henri Matisse, whose bold colors and lively patterns were well known to Glackens since he had seen them in the Armory Show in New York in 1913. Moreover, in addition to revisiting the curvilinear forms he

had experimented with in *Children Rollerskating*, Glackens may have been inspired to explore some of the structural concerns that occupied Paul Cézanne after he traveled through Aix-en-Provence and visited the Cézanne museum there before settling in La Ciotat for the summer.[56]

This work and others dating from Glackens's last summers in France met with wide critical acclaim when shown at Kraushaar Galleries in New York in the spring of 1931. Most notably, regarding claims that Glackens was too slavish a follower of Renoir, the critic in *Art News* wrote, "Mr. Glackens has dwelt contentedly for so long within the pleasant limits of the Renoir tradition that it is something of a surprise as well as a plea-sure to note that he is emerging ... from his adopted and adapted style into something more genuinely his own. And I should unhesitatingly put down these new Glackens landscapes as the best work that he has ever shown."[57]

Another critic noted that "Mr. Glackens has been painting through France ... with a freshness, a beauty of color, a simplicity of composition, closely in accord with his repu-tation as a man who feels color keenly and an artist of profound sensitiveness." When she went on to praise his "power to drench a canvas in sunlight,"[58] she could certainly have been looking at *Bowlers, La Ciotat*, as could the critic who observed that "seldom has the blazing sunlight and oppressive heat of the South of France been better recorded in paints on canvas. Just to look at them makes one feel the languor of hot places."[59]

21 Bay Shore, 1931

Oil on canvas. 14 × 22 inches. Gift of C. Richard Hilker. 2001.10.1

Like his earlier paintings *House in Conway* and *Along the Marne* (see pls. 17, 20), *Bay Shore* depicts a locale where Glackens happily vacationed with his family, and it too represents his Impressionist landscape painting style, filled with verve.[60] All three paintings emphasize light, as did the Impressionist masterworks Glackens so admired. In these paintings the artist conveyed the warm sun found in the heat of summer and the respites from the heat available in cool shadows along the water.

Bay Shore was painted during Glackens's last summer in France with his family at Villa des Orangers in Le Suquet near Cannes. In describing the summer accommodations, Ira Glackens wrote: "on the hill known as Le Suquet, in the old quarter of town, a most curious little villa was discovered. It was built like an arch, and a gate went right through the middle of it, leading into the grounds of the Pension des Orangers. The living quarters of the Villa des Orangers were upstairs … when it came to the choice, the G.'s always found themselves inhabiting the curious house." Despite the peculiar domestic arrangement, Glackens produced several exceptional works, among them *Fête du Suquet* (Whitney Museum of American Art, New York). Ira noted that it "preserves the spirit of Cannes in the summer, the blinding light, the burning heat, and the carefree populace."[61] *Bay Shore* also captures the carefree spirit of summer in Cannes, showing people on the shore, making ready to embark on an excursion, a leisurely boat ride that would take them away from the stifling heat to enjoy cool breezes on the water. *Bay Shore* was preceded by a drawing in a sketchbook (fig. 34) that depicts the locale before the people shown enjoying it in the finished oil were added.

Like *Bowlers, La Ciotat* painted the year before (see pl. 20), Glackens once again used vibrant complementary colors to enliven the scene, most notably the turquoise green that appears on the boathouse roof and the golden yellow with flecks of orange that colors the back of the boat. The treetops are also painted with the same dappled, emerald green strokes seen in the earlier work.

Fig. 34 Preparatory drawing for *Bay Shore* (2001.10.1) in "W. Glackens Bay Shore" (sketchbook), 1931. Charcoal on paper. 8½ × 5¼ inches. Gift of the Sansom Foundation 94.116

22 Back of Nude, c. 1930s

Oil on canvas. 30 × 25 inches. Bequest of Ira Glackens. 92.34

The figure in *Back of Nude* was a studio model Glackens hired to pose for him, yet in the nuance of her pose and gesture he conveyed a sense of her lived experience. As in *Breakfast Porch* (see pl. 18), Glackens again suggests some aspect of the emotional life of his subject. Although the artist painted many nudes in his career, as Matthew Baigell noted, "the personalities of his sitters are invariably individual and singular. In this regard Glackens responded to the things of this world rather than relying on a system of brushstrokes of spectral colors, however informally applied, in order to bring his painting to life." And, in Glackens's nudes,

> Critics and historians have often noted the influence of Renoir on these works. While it is true that elements of Renoir's palette are present, Glackens' intentions appear to be quite different from those of the French artist. Where Renoir's subjects remained as studio models often lacking individual personalities, Glackens caught something in the poses and facial features that reflected the model's mood or personality.... he ultimately gave his sitters distinctly unique rather than generically bland temperaments.

In Glackens's work, a depiction of a nude can become "a portrait of a state of mind."[62]

Unlike his two most famous nudes, *Girl with Apple* (see fig. 36) and *Temple Gold Medal Nude*, so named after it was awarded the prestigious Temple Gold Medal at the Pennsylvania Academy of the Fine Arts in 1924,[63] *Back of Nude*, dating from the 1930s, provides a close-up view of the figure in a nondescript setting; the earlier works show the nude women in clearly defined interior spaces seated or reclining on furniture in the artist's studio with his canvases stacked or hanging nearby. In the earlier works the sitters acknowledge the viewer's presence; they either make eye contact or look demurely away. In *Back of Nude* we have come upon a figure unaware of our presence as she lets down her hair, perhaps after a bath. Moreover, while there is a faint suggestion of a dark curtain with fringe or tassels behind her, for the most part, the vague space surrounding her is composed solely of flurried brushstrokes that reflect or in some places match the colors of her hair and body.

The woman in *Back of Nude* enjoys a relaxed, private, tranquil moment, and that sentiment is expressed as much through the smooth, tactile quality of the paint and the colors used as by the model's pose and gesture. The languid sensuality of her body is accentuated through the long, feathered brushstrokes that describe her contours, and, in true modernist fashion and perhaps with inspiration from Henri Matisse, sinuous strokes of cool green paint define the arch of her back. The contrasting textures and colors, ranging from the smoothness of her warm cream skin, blended with tints of green and pink, to the rougher texture of her thick auburn hair, contribute to an image that richly captures an intimate, contemplative moment, a unique experience, a "portrait of a state of mind."

Glackens's Still-Life Paintings

Glackens's enthusiasm for recording the beauty he found in handsome figurative subjects, bustling urban scenes, and idyllic landscapes extended to artfully placed still-life subjects. The arrangements of flowers and bowls of fruit in decorative containers that appear in Glackens's early work, initially playing secondary roles in larger figurative compositions, soon came to the fore. He painted them often and exquisitely throughout his career, first exhibiting them in 1916 and producing more "floral portraits," or flower pieces, as they were known, than any other body of work. Late in his life, when his health was failing and he lacked the physical stamina required to complete larger paintings, "his still life and flower arrangements reflect his inability to venture too far from the comforts of home. But physical limitations did little to impede the lively nature of his art."[64] In the years leading up to his death in 1938, he created numerous small still-life compositions that are now counted among his finest works.

In 1936, two years before he died at age sixty-eight, Glackens was awarded a Garden Club Prize for a still life that was shown in the prestigious Carnegie International exhibition. "This honor was appropriate for his particular gift; no artist ever more deserved this recognition of his flower paintings. Forbes Watson has well noted that few artists of any period painted flowers more in the spirit in which the earth made them. He captured the essential qualities of the flowers that made them live perpetually enveloped in his luminous colors."[65] This flattering and astute observation, coming as it did from an influential art critic, was no doubt heartening to Glackens as evidence that his creative powers were not waning.

In the same way that the people, locales, and interior settings in his larger, more complex works often held personal meaning for Glackens, so, too, did his still-life subjects, often fruits the family enjoyed eating and flowers grown in the gardens near homes the family occupied. The containers that held the colorful fruits and varied blooms were also chosen either because they were favored objects the family owned or simply bowls, vases, or pitchers that the artist found inherently beautiful. Glackens preferred the casual placement of flowers within a vase or pitcher. He did not arrange them, choosing instead to let the flowers and foliage fall naturally; he believed that "the day after a bouquet of flowers was put in a vase, the flowers essentially arranged themselves, and, therefore, there was no need for the artist to adjust his still-life arrangement in any formal order."[66] Ira Glackens echoed this observation when he wrote, "I had never seen him put any flowers in a vase or arrange them. Usually, he would see a bunch of flowers in the living room, put there by my mother, and pick them up and carry them to his studio … sometimes my mother would 'plant' a vase of flowers and say nothing. Soon … it would be up in his studio being painted."[67]

Throughout his career, as Glackens worked on larger, more complex compositions, the same bold stylistic ventures that characterized his figurative, landscape, and interior

Fig. 35 *Portrait of the Artist's Wife*, 1904. Oil on canvas. 74⅝ × 39⅝ inches. Wadsworth Atheneum Museum of Art, Hartford, Connecticut, U.S.A. Photograph © Wadsworth Atheneum Museum of Art/Art Resource, NY. 1956.27

subjects were pursued in his still lifes as well. While staying true to the appearance of the natural forms of the objects portrayed, the still-life paintings display the same daring coloristic arrangements and lively brushwork found in his larger pictures. As his ongoing forays into Impressionist technique continued, the "influence of Renoir had delightful results in the small, sparkling flower pieces through which the purification and intensification of the artist's color may be traced."[68]

Two early examples of masterfully rendered still lifes appearing as secondary decorative elements in larger figurative compositions can be found in *Portrait of the Artist's Wife* (fig. 35), painted in 1904, the year of their marriage, and *Girl with Apple* (fig. 36)

Fig. 36 *Girl with Apple*, 1909–1910. Oil on canvas. 39⁷⁄₁₆ × 56³⁄₁₆ inches. Brooklyn Museum, Dick S. Ramsay Fund. 56.70

of 1909–1910, a signature work that inaugurated his full-fledged conversion to the style of the Impressionists.[69] Glackens clearly considered the still life an essential component of the painting now known as *Portrait of the Artist's Wife*, since when it was exhibited at the National Arts Club in 1908, he called it *Lady with Fruit*. Given the prominent placement of the fruit, which has been described as a "ravishingly painted fruit still life,"[70] and the fact that it provides the only bright notes of color in an otherwise earth-toned canvas, the title *Lady with Fruit* was an accurate one. Another early version of the title, *Lady with a Basket of Fruit*, which also acknowledges the significance of the fruit to the composition, may help to explain why, according to Ira Glackens, the work was rejected from a portrait exhibition. He recounted that in 1906 "'Portrait of the Artist's Wife,' originally called 'Lady with a Basket of Fruit,' had been rejected by the Society of American Artists for a portrait show, and the reason given was that the basket of fruit standing on a small table beside the full-length seated figure somehow took the painting out of the realm of portraiture. It was evidently a still life!" Juror Robert Henri "had made a row but to no avail."[71]

In *Girl with Apple*, painted six years later, a work that, like *At Mouquin's* (see fig. 5), has been widely heralded as among Glackens's finest, a fruit bowl is again placed prominently, here in the left foreground. It is given emphasis not only because the young woman has casually plucked an apple from the bowl but also because of the chromatic range evident in the fruits. The red apples are set off against the warm yellow fruits, and, directly in the center of the bowl, a bright green apple is placed so as to heighten the contrast and draw attention to the still life. The bowl of fruit is also painted with more precise detail than other parts of the painting, with the exception of the model's sullen face. In a work like this, it is easy to see that Glackens will soon make the leap to painting luscious still lifes that isolate and celebrate the beauty of the fruits and flowers he so enjoyed.

After Glackens had married and began to include family members in his figurative compositions, still-life arrangements found in his home were often prominently placed in his paintings. In works such as *Breakfast Porch*, 1925 (see pl. 18), which, as noted, was painted in two versions, and *Lenna Resting* (fig. 37), the still lifes in the foregrounds are almost larger than the figures next to or behind them. Moreover, in all three cases, more attention is lavished on the flowers than on the figures, and the space they occupy appears cramped, as if the vase or basket of flowers came first and the figures were then fit in around the still life.

Fig. 37 *Lenna Resting*, c. 1920. Oil on canvas. 25½ × 31½ inches. Private Collection, courtesy Berry-Hill Galleries, New York

23 Flowers on a Garden Chair, 1925

Oil on canvas. 15 × 20 inches. Bequest of Ira Glackens. 91.40.112

Flowers on a Garden Chair was painted in 1925 in Samois-sur-Seine, France, where the Glackens family spent the summer in a rented house called the Maison Daboncourt that, according to Ira Glackens, "had been built in the late seventeenth century; in the rear was a fine walled garden containing an *orangerie*."[72]

Painted at the same time as the *Breakfast Porch* (see pl. 18), which, as noted, displays spatial incongruities, in *Flowers on a Garden Chair* the viewpoint and delineation of space are oddly skewed as well. Glackens shows us what appears to be a profile view of the pitcher that holds the bouquet *and* an aerial view of the chair seat at the same time. This tilting of the chair seat—showing it as if seen from above when the pitcher is shown in profile, thereby deliberately ignoring the rules of linear perspective—was a spatial anomaly first used by Paul Cézanne in his still-life paintings, an example of which Glackens knew from the Armory Show of 1913.[73]

Glackens also had a penchant for using elevated viewpoints to impart visual clarity to his illustrations, early works in which he was establishing compositional structures that he would utilize for the rest of his life. With that said, Glackens may have intentionally skewed the perspective to show a more accurate view of the woven pattern of the chair seat—an appealing geometric design that is set off by the curvilinear lines of the chair back. Whatever his intentions, like Cézanne, he created spatial tension within the composition by tilting the chair seat so emphatically that it appears as if the pitcher of flowers might slide off.

Glackens's love for decorative detail extended to the rendering of the design on the distinctive French Quimper pitcher, which shows a man in profile dressed in a red shirt and blue trousers, standing next to a tree; the colors of his garments are repeated in the bouquet above. The palette features Glackens's favored emerald green on the metal chair as well as the shiny foliage in the bouquet, masterfully set off against the cool blue pitcher and bachelor buttons and the assorted deep red and vermilion blooms, with white daisies added for contrast.

Whatever his intent, and despite its spatial anomalies, the painting represents Glackens at his best. While spending his first delightful summer in France with his family, he portrayed the beauty of the garden setting and the furniture and flowers found within it. *Flowers on a Garden Chair* is an overtly cheerful picture, an example of what a critic had in mind when she wrote, "what joy in pure painting these flower pieces afford!"[74]

24 Plums in a Saucer, c. 1930s

Oil on canvas. 7¼ × 10½ inches. Bequest of Ira Glackens. 91.40.115

The composition and paint handling in this charming small oil probably represent yet another example of the inspiration Glackens found in his friendship with fellow modernist painter Maurice Prendergast. Once again, Ira Glackens's recollections provide us with an anecdote that might explain the source of influence. Ira recounted that

> Maurice came to visit the G.'s when we were spending the summer at Bellport, Long Island, in 1912. He brought his sketch box of course, and when everyone was sitting on the lawn under the trees one hot day he noticed a small bowl of fruit on the grass, got out his paints, and painted it [fig. 38]. He left the picture behind him, and we have always treasured it. In later years W. more than once spoke of the difficulty of painting those green apples against the green grass, and much admired the little painting. After Maurice's death Charles made one of his beautiful frames for it.[75]

While the brushwork in the Prendergast work, now known as *Apples and Pears on the Grass*, is choppier, it nonetheless displays the vigorous movement that Glackens employed when applying the paint in his *Plums in a Saucer*, especially evident in the diagonal sweeping strokes in the background and the larger swirling strokes that describe the green shadow behind the saucer. The smaller dabs of paint that define the round fruits echo the motion of the larger, more animated brushstrokes in the Prendergast, and the overall effect is similar, as are the palettes—both artists used bold juxtapositions of vivid complementary colors to enliven the surface of their pictures. For Glackens, the use of the green shadow may allude to the influence of Henri Matisse as well—the Fauve master was in the habit of painting shadows in complementary colors—and Glackens would do the same in his *Back of Nude*, dating from the same period (see pl. 22).

Fig. 38 Maurice Prendergast *Apples and Pears on the Grass*, 1912. Oil on board. 9½ × 13 inches. Bequest of Ira Glackens. 91.40.109

25 Flowers in a Quimper Pitcher, c. 1930

Oil on canvas. 24 × 18 inches. Bequest of Ira Glackens. 91.40.144

Glackens's first paintings of bouquets in distinctive French Quimper pottery, produced in the town of Quimper in Brittany since the early eighteenth century, date to about 1913–1915. The Barnes Foundation owns an example purchased directly from the artist. The Barnes picture shows a dark upright figure between two symmetrical floral motifs comparable to the floral motifs that create the pattern on the front of the Quimper pitcher that appears in the Museum of Art | Fort Lauderdale painting. *Flowers in a Quimper Pitcher*, painted when Glackens's health was beginning to fail, nonetheless "offers wonderful assurance that the master has not lost his touch, with the floral pattern on the lovely French pitcher (a favorite container for his still-life arrangements), an echo of the live flowers bursting above."[76]

Since Glackens painted many floral still lifes with Quimper pitchers that have not yet been thoroughly documented, it is not possible to distinguish which ones were exhibited or referenced in publications, but, as Ira described his father's last summer of painting, he singled out a Quimper pitcher picture as one of his best. He wrote that "the summer of 1937 was spent in a house some distance out of Stratford, Connecticut. It was a beautiful place, surrounded with peach orchards, lawns and flower beds … life there was very pleasant. It was a fine secluded spot." He then explained that, despite the bucolic setting, his father "painted little that year," but that "'Bouquet in Quimper Pitcher' was produced, the best-known and perhaps most gay and brilliant of all his many flower pieces."[77]

This late painting praised by Ira was the one described by a critic who wrote, regarding Glackens's transition from his early dark paintings to the brighter colors he used later in his career, "from then on he was committed to his glowing, vibrant, luminous study of form in color which he brought to a culmination in … *Bouquet in a Quimper Pitcher*."[78]

Quimper pottery most likely appealed to Glackens because of the variety of hand-painted motifs that cover their lustrous surfaces. The lively floral designs on the pottery in *Flowers in a Quimper Pitcher* trail up the front of the pitcher. The thin, quick strokes of deep red and vermilion on the pot lead the eye up to the lavish bouquet, where rich red, cream, and rose pink hues are set off against the lush dark green foliage.

Exuberant and beautifully crafted still-life paintings like this one may have been what Guy Pène du Bois had in mind when he wrote that Glackens painted "some of the most vibrant flower pieces known to our painting."[79] A critic who reviewed an exhibit that included Glackens's flower paintings in 1937 was equally effusive in her praise: "What lusciousness of pigment, what purity of color and astounding candor of statement."[80]

Fig. 39 *Soda Fountain*, 1935. Oil on canvas. 48 × 36 inches.
Pennsylvania Academy of the Fine Arts, Philadelphia,
Joseph E. Temple and Henry D. Gilpin Funds. 1955.3

26 Pineapple, 1935

Oil on canvas. 9½ × 12¼ inches. Bequest of Ira Glackens. 91.40.129

This small oil panel is another example of a study in the Museum of Art | Fort Lauderdale collection that sheds light on a larger masterwork. This charming pineapple has been dated to the 1930s, when still-life paintings occupied much of Glackens's time and energy. When he rarely had the physical stamina required to tackle the larger compositions he had painted in earlier years, he nonetheless managed to complete *The Soda Fountain* in 1935 (fig. 39), his last monumental figurative composition—and, just as Ira had appeared in *Family Group* twenty-five years earlier, he appeared again, aged twenty-eight, in *The Soda Fountain* as the model for the young man behind the counter.

In *The Soda Fountain*, the humble pineapple of the Museum of Art | Fort Lauderdale study is given prominence, sitting proudly atop the large, elaborate arrangement of citrus fruits on the counter. Given that the Ira Glackens bequest comprised the family's personal collection of work, it is tempting to suggest that Ira might have kept the study of the pineapple as a memento of *The Soda Fountain* and the role he played in its creation, painted three years before his father died.

27 White Rose and Other Flowers, 1937

Oil on canvas. 15 × 20 inches. Bequest of Ira Glackens. 91.40.148

White Rose and Other Flowers dates from the family's last summer together at their vacation home outside Stratford, Connecticut. After describing his father's Quimper pitcher painting, completed that summer, as "the most gay and brilliant of all his many flower pieces," Ira wrote that, sadly, Glackens painted "another smaller and more quiet flower piece, a little bouquet in a glass, standing on a pink lustre dish.... This proved to be W.G.'s last completed canvas."[81] As was so often the case in his earlier floral still lifes, the flowers had been picked from a garden on the property where they were staying. This "quiet flower piece" was exhibited in the *Sixth Annual Exhibition of Contemporary American Painting* at the Whitney Museum of American Art later in 1937.

The lively brushwork and varied textures do not suggest the work of an artist with diminished capacities, nor does the lush palette, filled as it is with bright oranges, golden yellows, and deep emerald greens. Moreover, the pigment is skillfully applied with a variety of strokes that suggest the forms they are describing—small, short strokes sweep upward to create the petals of the zinnias, while thicker strokes of white paint define the prominent white bloom that brightens the whole bouquet.

28 Untitled [Still Life with Paint Tubes], 1937–1938

Oil on board. 6¼ × 8½ inches. Gift of the Sansom Foundation. 92.27

After returning from their vacation in Connecticut to their home in New York City at summer's end in 1937, Ira described his father's continued decline, as he suffered from a worsening heart condition. "In the winter, back in the studio, his eyes bothered him more, headaches were frequent.... He puttered in his studio, painting a single flower or pear or apple on a scrap of canvas, and finally merely a little study of a half-squeezed tube of paint that happened to be lying on the table beside his easel. This was the last time he ever painted at all."[82]

Painted on a small wooden board, this poignant image is a tender memorial to the tools of Glackens's lifelong trade, harking back to his earliest efforts to record with paint the exuberance he found in the world around him. And while he may have been weakened physically, his visual acuity and his dexterity with a paintbrush had not suffered. The small translucent glass bottle that holds his turpentine or linseed oil is carefully rendered with highlights reflecting the play of light on the glass, and two of the paint tubes are perfectly foreshortened, creating the illusion of projecting into a nondescript three-dimensional space. The brushstrokes are as animated as any he ever put down, and the rose red and warm gold labels on his treasured paint tubes are luminous, as are the highlights on the metal surfaces. This modest panel is a touching last effort of a gifted artist, admired and respected by the public and his peers alike, one of whom praised his ability to share with his audience "above all ... the pleasure derived from just painting."[83]

Ira Glackens concludes his story about his father and "the artists who freed American art" by recounting his father's passing, explaining that while visiting his good friend and frame maker Charles Prendergast and his wife at their home in Westport, Connecticut, Glackens suffered a cerebral hemorrhage and quickly lost consciousness. His wife, Edith, later told a friend that "he died as peacefully as he lived."[84] Ira wrote, "I cannot think of a happier life than the one my father lived ... he had known the best that life has to offer: a peaceful nature, a devoted wife, a happy home, delightful friends, and the contentment that comes from creative work."[85]

When he heard of Glackens's death, the artist's dear lifelong friend Dr. Albert Barnes wrote to Edith, saying that he felt "a deep sorrow.... He was so *real*, and so gentle and of a character that I would have given millions to possess. And as an artist, I don't need to tell you I esteemed him ... he will live forever in the Foundation collection among the great painters of the past who, could they speak, would say he was one of the elect."[86]

29 Self-Portrait, 1900

Oil on canvas. 9 × 7 inches. Bequest of Ira Glackens. 91.40.10

This self-portrait was painted the year before Edith Dimock (1876–1955) met William Glackens, when she was studying with the American Impressionist painter William Merritt Chase at what was then known as the Chase School in New York City. She had first studied with Chase when he gave weekly classes near her home in Hartford, Connecticut, and eventually she convinced her family to allow her to move to New York, where she shared an apartment with a fellow art student at the Sherwood Studios, located near the school.

Although she was studying with Chase at the time, *Self-Portrait* is more akin stylistically to works by the followers of Robert Henri. Overall, the palette is muted and the tonalities are dark, but the luminous areas that emerge from the shadows are painted in lighter hues like those the French Impressionists favored. Ira Glackens later observed, "it can be seen that E., in spite of her early studies with William M. Chase, was unalterably herself and a born disciple of the Ashcan School. No wonder Chase said that he could not make her out, but he thought she was a genius."[87] Ira's assessment of her later work, which was executed primarily in watercolor, was shared by his father and echoed Chase's sentiments: "it seemed to me that her watercolors display so original and satirical a vision and style, that they cannot be compared to the work of anyone else. Father admired them very much even before they married."[88]

Clearly, the Glackenses had a two-artist marriage, readily acknowledged by Ira. He was proud of his mother's "original and satirical … vision and style" and praised her for the recognition she received and the profile she maintained as a respected artist in New York. He recounted that "her watercolors appeared in many group shows, going back to 1904. Many were shown at the Independents of 1910 exhibit and at the Armory show, where they all sold; in 1928 she was given a show at the Whitney Studio Club, forerunner of the Whitney Museum. The show was later invited to Chicago."[89]

Edith Dimock's watercolor style can best be described as combining gestural drawing with loose brushwork and a dark palette reminiscent of those of Édouard Manet and Henri—painted surfaces were then enlivened with overlays of more vibrant colors and animated drawn lines. The resulting images are lively vignettes, genre scenes often showing mothers and children, going about their daily routines in the American and French cities and towns where the Glackens family lived. As her husband had done in his illustrations and paintings, Dimock too recorded what she observed in urban and rural marketplaces and on street corners—women are shown shopping for food with children and baskets in tow, emphasizing their nurturing roles.

30 Rain, c. 1904

Watercolor on paper. 6½ × 8 inches. Bequest of Ira Glackens. 91.40.95

In his memoir, Ira recounted that in 1904, "E. had one of her watercolors accepted by the American Watercolor Society for its Spring exhibition and on May 3 a review appeared in the *Evening Sun* which, though unsigned, bore internal evidence of having come from the pen, or rather the quill, of Charles Fitzgerald." In response to *Rain* FitzGerald wrote, "There is mischief in this artist's work, ... Miss Dimock is not orthodox at all. She comes to her world very unconventionally, free from pictorial prejudice. ... Here is an artist with a definite aim, a keen fresh vision, readily interested in the humorous, whimsical aspect of her neighbors: ... And these little fragments are picked out with an astonishing eye to the essential features.... It is a wonderful art.... a picture comes that is a truer impression of life."[90]

31 Italian Fish Market, c. 1916

Watercolor on paper. 8¾ × 8½ inches. Bequest of Ira Glackens. 91.40.78

Like her husband, Edith Dimock Glackens often changed the titles of her watercolors when they were exhibited. The titles were usually descriptive, and she painted multiple versions of similar subjects, so while it is not always possible to discern precisely which sheets were exhibited, published remarks sometimes provide clues. For example, a reference to "a glimpse of a fish market" in a review of an exhibition in 1916 at the Thumb Box Gallery may well refer to this watercolor or one like it. Also, this exhibition included works by both William and Edith; however, Edith always used her maiden name when she exhibited her work. A March 1916 *American Art News* review reads, "E. Dimock handles watercolor cleverly in a group of impressions of east side life, the best of which is probably a glimpse of a fish market."[91]

Both artists had also exhibited works, New York City views, in the 1911 annual exhibition of the American Watercolor Society, mounted in New York and later shown at the Art Institute of Chicago. When the exhibit was reviewed in the *Brooklyn Daily Eagle*, with the subtitle "Strong in Individuality," the reviewer noted that "W. Glackens' 'East Side' far outweighs his 'Washington Square' ... and that 'East Ninth Street at Noon,' and 'Street Group' by E. Dimock, for glaring color might be repudiated even by the post-impressionists."[92]

32 Epicerie, 1925

Watercolor on paper. 7 × 9¼ inches. Bequest of Ira Glackens. 91.40.200

33 Going to Market, 1926

Watercolor on board. 8 × 9½ inches. Bequest of Ira Glackens. 91.40.133

These two works were painted in France when the Glackens family was living in either Samois-sur-Seine or Vence. These watercolors, or others like them, were most likely among the works mentioned by critics who reviewed Dimock's 1928 exhibition at the Whitney Studio Club.

The critic for the *New York Times* wrote, "A lively show of watercolors by Edith Dimock … opened at the Whitney Studio Club. Miss Dimock has taken the plunge into provincial France, and come out with a delightful collection of glimpses into the comédie humaine," with "ruddy butter-and-egg women, school children and café loungers.… 'The Egg Market' is a genuine pictorial achievement."[93]

The Whitney Studio Club exhibition was most favorably reviewed by the critic writing in *Art News*, who praised Dimock's efforts while at the same time alluding to the "fifty-odd sketches" on display—a large number of works that indicates how prolific she was during her years abroad. Effusive in his or her praise, the critic wrote:

> Seldom has the passing Parisian and provincial show been recorded as trenchantly as by Miss Dimock in her fifty-odd sketches of "some of the people in France." And seldom in so numerous an assortment of water colors by the same hand does one find so little sameness. So large a pageant of peasants, *pensionnaires*, priests and *boulevardieres* … as the collection lacks a single dull or repetitious piece, selection is difficult. Careful consideration leads us to list the following as among the very wittiest and best: In the Square B, Spring Flowers, Butter and Eggs A and B, Orphan Girls and Boys … at the Midnight Mass A and B, Retail egg Market … Number 52 is ominously entitled "The End." For the present show only, we hope. These are, according to our catalog, only "Some of the people in France." And until we have them all … we shall, like undaunted Oliver Twists, continue to ask for more.[94]

Although on a more modest scale, as late as 1934, four years before her husband died, Edith Dimock was still exhibiting her work, but by this time, she was referred to by her married name as well. A *New York Times* notice read, "Water-colors by Edith Dimock (Mrs. William J. Glackens) are on view at the Charlton House Studio of Elizabeth Anne Frank, 41 Charlton Street. They include French Market scenes and two impressions of 'Four Saints in Three Acts.'"[95] The twenty-four-year-old "genius" student of William Merritt Chase was still eagerly sharing her "original and satirical … vision" at the age of fifty-eight.

John Sloan

There are twenty prints by John Sloan (1871–1951) in the Glackens Collection, more works by anyone other than William and Edith Glackens and Glackens's brother Louis, attesting to the lifelong friendship that Sloan and Glackens shared. They had known each other since high school in Philadelphia, where they both began drawing for newspapers, and, after the two moved to New York City to pursue careers as artists, they gained notoriety when they exhibited in the famed exhibition of the Eight in 1908. They remained close in the decades thereafter.

The five etchings selected for discussion here are of particular interest because they were produced as part of a series entitled New York City Life, created in 1905–1906, when Sloan, like Glackens, had tried to capture as directly as possible truthful vignettes of daily life as he observed it in New York City. There were ten prints in the original series, intended to be sold as reasonably priced complete sets that Sloan hoped would sell briskly. "The prints represent all classes of people and many kinds of urban activity.... These were his finest technical achievements to date. The tone is sometimes satirical, but it is not harsh or unjust. The scenes are in response to the energy of New York, to its continuous activity and variety, but Sloan saw the private and tranquil moments as well. Certainly the series represents one of the most successful efforts by an artist to capture New York City's variety and movement."[96]

Helen Farr Sloan, the artist's widow, shared her husband's feelings about the inspiration he found when they moved to New York City. He said, "I saw the life of the city really for the first time.... Coming to New York and finding a place to live where I could observe the backyards and rooftops behind our attic studio—it was a new and exciting experience.... New York had its human comedy and I felt like making pictures of this everyday world.... I saw neighborhoods of the city, and saw the kind of people who lived, worked and played.... On the whole, when finding incidents that provided ideas for paintings, I was selecting bits of joy in human life."[97]

The etchings discussed below are numbered in accordance with their sequence in the original series, and some of the captions written by the artist, decades after the etchings were created, are included. After his death, when Sloan's New York prints were published, Helen Farr Sloan included the captions when they were exhibited in a retrospective exhibition. She quoted him as having said that "in providing comments for the various pictures in this collection I shall endeavor to return to the mood under which they were produced."[98]

JOHN SLOAN

34 Connoisseurs of Prints, 1905

Etching on woven paper. 5½ × 7½ inches. Bequest of Ira Glackens. 91.40.72

This image can be seen as a biting, satirical commentary on customers perusing prints for sale in a crowded art gallery, perhaps expressing Sloan's resentment that, despite his best efforts, his own prints met with limited commercial success; he may be mocking the "connoisseurs" who so often rejected his work. The two most prominent prospective buyers in the picture are not depicted in a flattering fashion: a large scowling man in the center clearly has much to say, no doubt voicing an opinion, yet he barely looks at the art on the wall in front of him, while a haughty man on the right scrutinizes a print with a magnifying glass. One "connoisseur" does not appear to look at the prints at all, while the other focuses on minutiae. In his caption Sloan identified the setting of this image as "the Old American Art Galleries on 23rd Street."

35 Fifth Avenue Critics, 1905

Also known as *Connoisseurs of Virtue* and *Une Rue à New York*. Etching on paper, watermarked.
5½ × 7½ inches. Bequest of Ira Glackens. 91.40.80

Here Sloan is commenting on the behaviors of upper-class people, women in particular, who have appointed themselves "connoisseurs of virtue," in this case, passing judgment on the young woman shown, and surely on everyone else whom they will pass by. "In … *Fifth Avenue Critics*, Sloan found the rich worthy of more cutting criticism.… [he] contrasts the reactions of two elderly, affluent women as their carriage passes another with a young woman passenger, who is beautiful and elegantly dressed. One of the older women responds with a warm smile.… Her companion's reaction is stiff, upright, and disapproving.… What is clear is her arrogance and mean-spiritedness."[99]

36 Man Monkey, 1905

Etching on laid paper. 5 × 7 inches. Bequest of Ira Glackens. 91.40.88

Sloan's caption reads: "In the side streets of the Chelsea and Greenwich Village districts, the one-man band with hand-organ accompanist furnished free entertainment to those who dropped no pennies. He worried the horse-drawn traffic of the time, but before many years the automobile and motor truck cleared him from the streets."

37 Fun, One Cent, 1905

Etching on laid paper. 5½ × 7¼ inches. Bequest of Ira Glackens. 91.40.71

Sloan's caption reads: "The Nickelodeon [penny arcade], with its hand-cranked moving photographs, was one of the attractions preceding moving-picture theaters. The one in which I garnered this bouquet of laughing girls was for many years on Fourteenth Street near Third Avenue."

As part of a discussion about the emergence of commercial leisure, it has been noted that *Fun, One Cent* chronicles "a part of turn-of-the-century New York when the city became the capital of a new business—the leisure industry. Gradual decreases in working hours, the loosening of Victorian restraints, and the need for recreation … fueled a growing demand for leisure.… In … *Fun, One Cent* … three young women stand in a penny arcade, about to put a penny in a slot, turn a crank, and glimpse 'Those Naughty Chorus Girls.'"[100]

38 Turning Out the Light, 1905

Etching on woven Rives paper, watermarked. 5½ × 7½ inches. Bequest of Ira Glackens. 91.40.81

Sloan's caption reads: "This plate has 'charm': a verdict handed down by a very well-known art critic of those days, Russell Sturgis, to whom I showed this group of my New York etchings. Perhaps it has; I'm not interested … I presented him with a set of ten. He kept this print and returned the rest, breaking up a set. I was really furious at the time."

This etching is one of four from the New York City Life series that were deemed "vulgar" and therefore rejected by the American Watercolor Society for a May 1906 exhibition.[101] It represents one of the views that Sloan could have seen from his windows in a crowded part of the city, where many windows overlooked neighboring buildings. This image captures a tranquil moment, but since it alludes to an intimate relationship, it was considered unacceptable to the exhibition jury—it was, however, embraced by critics and the public alike.

"Perhaps his most provocative early works were the series of etchings he began in 1905, transcribing views … which he saw from the window of his studio on the edge of the Tenderloin district. His images of lower-class New Yorkers sleeping on rooftops on hot summer nights, prostitutes, and young girls enjoying naughty nickelodeon images were nonetheless enthusiastically received by New York critics."[102] Clearly, they and the public who embraced the pictures were pleased with Sloan's efforts to record, as his friend Glackens did, "the bits of joy in human life" that he had "selected."[103]

NOTES

1. H. E. Schnakenberg, "Exhibitions: William Glackens," *Arts* 17 (April 1931): 579–81.
2. Avis Berman, "Master of Delight: William J. Glackens at the Museum of Art, Fort Lauderdale," *Magazine Antiques* 178, no. 6 (November–December 2011): 1; and John O'Connor Jr., "The Glackens Exhibition," *Carnegie Magazine* 12 (February 1939): 277.
3. Leslie Katz, *William Glackens in Retrospect* (Saint Louis: City Art Museum of Saint Louis, 1966), n.p.
4. O'Connor, "The Glackens Exhibition," p. 277.
5. William H. Gerdts, "The Illustrator," in William H. Gerdts and Jorge H. Santis, *William Glackens* (Fort Lauderdale: Museum of Art; New York: Abbeville Press, 1996), p. 34.
6. [Mary Fanton Roberts?], "Foremost American Illustrators: Vital Significance of Their Work," *Craftsman* 17 (December 1909): 267.
7. Everett Shinn, "William Glackens as an Illustrator," *American Artist* 9 (November 1945): 22.
8. For a thorough overview of Glackens's work as an illustrator, see Nancy E. Allyn, "The Illustrations of William Glackens," in Allyn and Elizabeth H. Hawkes, *William Glackens: Illustrator in New York, 1897–1919* (Wilmington: Delaware Art Museum, 1985). Regarding those in the Museum of Art | Fort Lauderdale collection, see Gerdts, "The Illustrator," pp. 27–35.
9. Ira Glackens, *William Glackens and the Ashcan Group* (New York: Crown, 1957), rpt. as *William Glackens and the Eight: The Artists Who Freed American Art* (New York: Writers and Readers Publishing, 1990), pp. 23–24.
10. Clipping, "The Press: Reporters on the Brush," *Time Magazine*, October 29, 1945.
11. Clipping, "Art: Cavalcade," *Time Magazine*, July 17, 1950.
12. [Charles FitzGerald], "Art Notes," *New York Evening Sun*, April 11, 1901, p. 4.
13. Glackens, *William Glackens and the Eight*, p. 56.
14. "Pictures by American Artists Admired on 'Varnishing Day,'" *New York World*, March 24, 1905, p. 7: "Whistler has dominated the show and his influence is apparent on every side.... This is shown in a full length portrait of a young man by W. Glackens." William H. Gerdts has also noted the similarity between Glackens's portrait of FitzGerald and comparable works by Robert Henri, in "New York Scenes," in Gerdts and Santis, *William Glackens*, pp. 56–57.
15. For more detailed information about the Prendergast brothers' frame business, see Suzanne Smeaton, "Embracing Realism: Frames of the Ashcan Painters, 1895–1925," in James W. Tottis et al., *Life's Pleasures: The Ashcan Artist's Brush with Leisure, 1895–1925* (London: Merrell, 2007), p. 94.
16. Marilee Boyd Meyer, foreword to *Inspiring Reform: Boston's Arts and Crafts Movement*, ed. Marilee Boyd Meyer (Wellesley, Mass.: Davis Museum and Cultural Center, Wellesley College, 1997), p. 14.
17. Ira and William Glackens Papers, 1901–1990, card index of William Glackens's paintings, Archives of American Art, Smithsonian Institution.
18. Judith Barter et al., *American Arts at the Art Institute of Chicago: From Colonial Times to World War I* (Chicago: Art Institute of Chicago, 1998), p. 322.
19. Ibid.
20. Judith Zilczer, "The Eight on Tour, 1908–1909," *American Art Journal* 16, no. 3 (Summer 1984): 30.
21. Glackens, *William Glackens and the Eight*, pp. 69–71. In the book he refers to his parents, William and Edith Glackens, as "W.G." and "E.G." and also as just "W." and "E."

22. Carol Nathanson, *Tracing Vision: Modern Drawings from the Georgia Museum of Art* (Athens: Georgia Museum of Art, 2011), p. 123.

23. For a thorough discussion of Glackens's illustrations of city scenes, see Rebecca Zurier, "William Glackens and the Legible City," in *Picturing the City: Urban Vision and the Ashcan School* (Berkeley: University of California Press, 2006), pp. 181–212, and essays by Rebecca Zurier, Robert W. Snyder, and Virginia M. Mecklenburg in *Metropolitan Lives: The Ashcan Artists and Their New York* (Washington, D.C.: National Museum of American Art, in association with W.W. Norton and Company, 1995).

24. Zurier, "William Glackens and the Legible City," p. 193.

25. Louise Eberle, "Penny Poisons: Some of the Things a Child's Cent May Buy from Unscrupulous Street Venders," *Collier's*, July 8, 1911, pp. 18–19.

26. Rebecca Zurier and Robert W. Snyder, introduction to Zurier, Snyder, and Mecklenburg, *Metropolitan Lives: The Ashcan Artists and Their New York*, p. 22.

27. Zurier, *Picturing the City: Urban Vision and the Ashcan School*, p. 209.

28. John Russell, "Art: When Glackens Illustrated for a Living," *New York Times*, August 13, 1982.

29. Ralph Minard, "Art Show Recalls Historic Home: Atheneum Displays Paintings of and by Former Occupants of Vanderbilt Mansion," *Hartford Times*, June 16, 1956, n.p.

30. Glackens, *William Glackens and the Eight*, pp. 184–85.

31. Zurier, *Picturing the City: Urban Vision and the Ashcan School*, p. 211, explains that "Most of Glackens's other city pictures employ a similar perspective, whether looking out over Wall Street [or] down onto the shoppers thronging Madison Square.... In his drawings of crowds, the elevated vantage point worked ... to clarify or individuate figures."

32. Peter John Brownlee, "On a Perpetual Holiday: The Art of William Glackens after the Eight," in *The Eight and American Modernisms*, ed. Elizabeth Kennedy (Chicago: University of Chicago Press, for Terra Foundation for American Art, 2009), p. 45.

33. John O'Connor Jr., "The Glackens Exhibition," *Carnegie Magazine* 12 (February 1939): 277.

34. Scott I. Walker and Robin E. Walker, *Postcard History Series: Dennis* (Charleston, S.C.: Arcadia Publishing, 2007), pp. 16–17. The pier was removed when "the hotel was dismantled in the 1930's, and as was common in the day, most all materials were saved and reused. Several houses on and about Scarsdale Road in Dennis were constructed ... with timbers and materials salvaged from the hotel." Walker and Walker, p. 17. I am grateful to Burton Derrick, Librarian at the Dennis Historical Society, Dennis, Massachusetts, for his kind assistance in providing me with archival photographs and documents from the Historical Society collection. The information he shared made it possible to confirm the Nobscussett Hotel location where *Cape Cod Pier* was painted and where the Glackens family stayed during the summer of 1908. I also thank Stephen Borkowski, Chair of the Provincetown Art Commission, Provincetown, Massachusetts, for sharing his abundant knowledge of the history and geography of Cape Cod.

35. Richard J. Wattenmaker, *American Paintings and Works on Paper in the Barnes Foundation* (Merion, Pa.: Barnes Foundation, 2010), pp. 76–78.

36. In his recent *American Paintings and Works on Paper in the Barnes Foundation*, Richard Wattenmaker wrote (pp. 66–67): "When he bought *Race Track* from Folsom Galleries in March 1913, Barnes was expressing his need to possess the talisman that had initiated him into what he came to see as a new world of perception and meaning. *Race Track* was for Barnes always primus inter pares, the centerpiece of his collection, its indispensability a deeply personal touchstone and perpetual tribute to Glackens."

37. Arthur Hoeber, "Art and Artists," *Globe and Commercial Advertiser*, April 5, 1910, p. 10.

38. Mary Fanton Roberts, "Notes of General Interest: Art in New York This Season," *Craftsman* 24 (April 1913): 136.

39. James Huneker, "Seen in the World of Art: William Glackens Shows His Versatility," *New York Sun*, December 18, 1910.

40. Mary Fanton Roberts, "Speaking of Art: W. J. Glackens Annual Show," *Arts and Decoration*, March 1931, p. 45.

41. William H. Gerdts, "New York Scenes," in Gerdts and Santis, *William Glackens*, pp. 66–67.

42. See Jorge H. Santis, "Introduction," in Gerdts and Santis, *William Glackens*, p. 180, for a discussion of *Children Rollerskating* in relation to other decorative works in the collection.

43. *Exhibition of Paintings, Drawings and Sculpture*, Montross Gallery, New York, March 23–April 25, 1915. Also "The 'Very Latest' at Montross Gallery," *American Art News*, March 27, 1915.

44. Vincent J. de Gregorio, "The Life and Art of William J. Glackens" (Ph.D. diss., Ohio State University, 1955), p. 256n1 quotes a letter from Ira Glackens, February 24, 1955: "when we lived at 29 Washington Square, we needed a new lampshade for a large standing lamp. Shades were very expensive as well as hideous in those days, so father undertook to paint one. I remember he got some books on Hindu mythology out of the library … and painted scenes from it around the lampshade…. Father was totally disinterested in religion or theology, and the Hindu subjects were investigated purely for their pictorial possibilities."

45. Brownlee, "On a Perpetual Holiday: The Art of William Glackens after the Eight," pp. 47–48.

46. Glackens, *William Glackens and the Eight*, pp. 195, 193–95.

47. Ibid., pp. 193–94, 194, 193.

48. Glackens painted another smaller version of *Breakfast Porch* (private collection), dated to 1920, but, given that the room depicted has the same green shutters visible in the larger version painted at Samois-sur-Seine in 1925, and the fact that the Glackenses summered in Conway, New Hampshire, in 1920, both paintings must date from 1925. The smaller painting shows only Glackens's daughter, Lenna, at the table with the same basket filled with a different bouquet. She appears to be wide awake as she looks at a single flower she holds in her hand, and in this composition the basket is very large, almost as big as the child.

49. Glackens, *William Glackens and the Eight*, p. 199.

50. William H. Gerdts, "The Late Work," in Gerdts and Santis, *William Glackens*, p. 147.

51. As noted by Richard J. Wattenmaker, *The Art of William Glackens* (New York: New York University, 1972), pp. 133–34, and in his *American Paintings and Works on Paper in the Barnes Foundation*, p. 73: "the artist and his wife may be seen, at the right of the canvas, watching the crowd…. These family figures in the Dieppe and other canvases, though small, are always characteristic, and can be identified at once."

52. Glackens, *William Glackens and the Eight*, pp. 42–44.

53. Ibid., p. 41.

54. Ibid., pp. 244–45.

55. Kenneth E. Silver, "The Mediterranean Muse: Artists on the Riviera between the Wars," in *Impressions of the Riviera: Monet, Renoir, Matisse and Their Contemporaries* (Portland, Maine: Portland Museum of Art, 1998), pp. 41, 43.

56. Glackens, *William Glackens and the Eight*, p. 244.

57. "William Glackens: Kraushaar Galleries," *Art News*, April 18, 1931, p. 10.

58. Mary Fanton Roberts, "Speaking of Art: W. J. Glackens Annual Show," *Arts and Decoration* 34 (March 1931): 45.

59. H. E. Schnakenberg, "Exhibitions: William Glackens," *Arts* 17 (April 1931): 579–81.

60. Unlike the bulk of the William Glackens collection at the Museum of Art | Fort Lauderdale, *Bay*

Shore was not part of the Ira Glackens bequest, nor was it a gift from the Sansom Foundation. In 2001 C. Richard Hilker, a museum trustee and close friend and adviser to Ira Glackens, bequeathed it to the museum.

61. Glackens, *William Glackens and the Eight*, pp. 249–50.

62. Matthew Baigell, Sotheby's, New York, *American Paintings, Drawings and Sculpture*, May 19, 2011, commentary for lot 28.

63. See ibid. for a reproduction.

64. Brownlee, "On a Perpetual Holiday: The Art of William Glackens after the Eight," p. 50.

65. John O'Connor Jr., "The Glackens Exhibition," *Carnegie Magazine* 12 (February 1939): 275.

66. De Gregorio, "The Life and Art of William J. Glackens," p. 231, includes the recollection of Mrs. George W. Bellows, wife of Glackens's friend, recorded during the author's interview with her in New York City, November 8, 1954.

67. Ira Glackens, letter, August 24, 1954, quoted in ibid., pp. 231–32.

68. Martha Davidson, "The Gay Glackens: In Memorium," *Art News* 37 (December 17, 1938): n.p.

69. When the Brooklyn Museum purchased *Girl with Apple* in 1958, John Gordon observed that "it is with 'Nude with Apple' [*Girl with Apple*] that he [Glackens] finally emerged as a confirmed disciple of Renoir whose style was so suited to his own warm and pleasant nature," in "Nude with Apple," *Brooklyn Museum Bulletin* 19 (Winter 1958): 6–9. Additional examples of prominent still lifes appearing in larger figurative works include *Family Group*, 1910–1911 (see fig. 20), and *The Artist's Wife and Son*, 1911 (Snite Museum of Art, University of Notre Dame, Notre Dame, Ind.), among others.

70. William H. Gerdts, "New York Scenes," in Gerdts and Santis, *William Glackens*, p. 59.

71. Glackens, *William Glackens and the Eight*, p. 77.

72. Ibid., p. 199.

73. A discussion of the influence of Cézanne on Glackens can be found in Wattenmaker, *American Paintings and Works on Paper in the Barnes Foundation*, p. 68.

74. Margaret Bruening, "Glackens and Schnakenberg," *American Magazine of Art* 30 (February 1937): 117. The 1937 Kraushaar exhibit included a room devoted exclusively to Glackens's floral still lifes.

75. Glackens, *William Glackens and the Eight*, p. 120.

76. Gerdts, "The Late Work," in Gerdts and Santis, *William Glackens*, p. 150.

77. Glackens, *William Glackens and the Eight*, p. 258.

78. John O'Connor Jr., "The Glackens Exhibition," *Carnegie Magazine* 12 (February 1939): 277.

79. Guy Pène du Bois, *Artists Say the Silliest Things* (New York: American Artist's Group, 1940), pp. 83–84.

80. Margaret Bruening, "Glackens and Schnakenberg," *American Magazine of Art* 30 (February 1937): 117.

81. Glackens, *William Glackens and the Eight*, p. 258.

82. Ibid., pp. 258–59.

83. H. E. Schnakenberg, "Exhibitions: William Glackens," *Arts* 17 (April 1931): 579.

84. Quoted in Glackens, *William Glackens and the Eight*, p. 259.

85. Ibid., p. 260.

86. Quoted in ibid.

87. Ibid., p. 58.

88. Ira Glackens, *Ira on Ira: A Memoir* (New York: Tenth Avenue Editions, 1992), p. 3.

89. Ibid.

90. Quoted in Glackens, *William Glackens and the Eight*, pp. 57–58.

91. "Group Exhibits at Thumb Box Gallery," *American Art News*, March 1916, p. 2.

92. "Watercolor Exhibit by American Society," *Brooklyn Daily Eagle*, May 1, 1911, p. 6.

93. "Edith Dimock and Beulah Stevenson at the Whitney Studio Club," *New York Times*, February 19, 1928, n.p. "The Egg Market" may be *Women with Eggs*, owned by the Barnes Foundation, or a watercolor very similar to it. For reproductions of *Women with Eggs* and three other watercolors by Dimock, see Wattenmaker, *American Paintings and Works on Paper in the Barnes Foundation*, pp. 331–33. Wattenmaker notes that these watercolors by Dimock are identical in style to works by her that were sold at the famed Armory Show in 1913. Dimock sold all of the eight watercolors she exhibited, but six of them were titled simply *Group*. See also Milton W. Brown, *The Story of the Armory Show*, 2nd ed. (New York: Abbeville Press; Joseph H. Hirshhorn Foundation, 1988), p. 262.

94. "In New York: Edith Dimock, Beulah Stevenson at the Whitney Studio Club," *Art News*, February 25, 1928, n.p.

95. "ART: Dimock Water-colors Shown," *New York Times*, March 29, 1934, n.p.

96. James Kraft, *John Sloan, A Printmaker* (Washington, D.C.: International Exhibition Foundation, 1984), p. 9.

97. Helen Farr Sloan, *John Sloan, New York Etchings (1905–1949)* (New York: Dover Publications, 1978), p. viii.

98. Ibid., p. x.

99. Robert W. Snyder and Rebecca Zurier, "Picturing the City," in Zurier, Snyder, and Mecklenburg, *Metropolitan Lives: The Ashcan Artists and Their New York*, p. 112.

100. Ibid., pp. 157, 156.

101. David W. Scott and E. John Bullard, *John Sloan, 1871–1951* (Washington, D.C.: National Gallery of Art, 1971), p. 87.

102. Virginia M. Mecklenburg, "Manufacturing Rebellion: The Ashcan Artists and the Press," in Zurier, Snyder, and Mecklenburg, *Metropolitan Lives: The Ashcan Artists and Their New York*, p. 201.

103. Helen Farr Sloan, *John Sloan, New York Etchings (1905–1949)* (New York: Dover Publications, 1978), p. viii.

ACKNOWLEDGMENTS

Working on this Glackens Collection publication for the Museum of Art | Fort Lauderdale, Nova Southeastern University has been a delight. As a fourth-generation New Yorker, I have always felt a personal rapport with his work. Indeed, I love his paintings of Central Park and Washington Square Park for their sheer beauty, and also because I was certain that the young women depicted in them must have been much like my dear grandmother in her youth.

Therefore, I could not be more grateful to Irvin Lippman, former director of the Museum of Art | Fort Lauderdale, for entrusting me with the task of writing this guide to its Glackens Collection. He and curator Jorge Hilker Santis, to whom I also express my gratitude for sharing invaluable information and ideas, were and are proud stewards of the works in their care, and I am honored to be welcomed into their fold. I also thank Avis Berman, an esteemed and generous colleague, for her guidance and advice as my work proceeded.

At the Museum of Art | Fort Lauderdale, Director of Exhibitions and Curatorial Services Rachel Talent Ivers and her knowledge of the Glackens Collection were essential to my research, as were the tireless efforts of Rachel A. Diana, Registrar of Collections, and Carrie Peterson, Collections and Records Associate; their professionalism and cheerful dispositions made my work at the Museum a pleasure. I am also indebted to Emily Wood, the resourceful curatorial assistant, who amassed many, many pages of crucial Glackens research materials; it would not have been possible to complete the text without her help.

At the Whitney Museum of American Art in New York, I thank the staff at the Frances Mulhall Achilles Library. Carol Rusk, Benjamin and Irma Weiss Librarian, and Kristen Leipert, Assistant Archivist, generously provided assistance in locating obscure exhibition records and reproductions of Glackens's work. I am also grateful to Burton Derrick, Librarian at the Dennis Historical Society, for sharing archival photographs and documents from their collection. Stephen Borkowski, Chair of the Provincetown Art Commission, helped me to discover the previously unknown location in Dennis, Massachusetts, where Glackens's groundbreaking and much-loved *Cape Cod Pier* was painted in 1908. He also reviewed the text, providing welcome observations and suggestions, as did Maria DeAngelis. Each of them truly has the art spirit, and I thank them both wholeheartedly. I am also grateful to Steven P. Hollman.

My goal from the outset of this project was to select and highlight works from the Glackens Collection that are exemplary for both their aesthetic merit and their historical significance and to present them to the reader with clarity and enthusiasm. If I have achieved that goal in even small measure, it is largely due to the efforts of my editor, Fronia W. Simpson. At every turn, she subtly sharpened my thinking and my language with eloquence and aplomb, and for her efforts and insights I am most thankful. I am also deeply grateful to Michael Russem, our masterful designer who cheerfully tackled the complex layout of this book, producing a handsome publication that honors the art works it presents and the efforts of all who contributed to it.

Last, I thank my eldest brother, Tom, a longtime fellow New York City resident, who was coincidentally for many years a bartender at McSorleys Old Ale House, a favored Greenwich Village haunt of the Ashcan painters a century ago. My brother always cherished the gift that he found everyday life in our fair city to be, and he inspired me and his beloved fifth-generation New Yorker nieces, Meaghan, Katie, and Mary Margaret, to feel the same. For that ebullient sentiment, often shared by Glackens and embodied in his views of New York, we will always be grateful.

Elizabeth Thompson Colleary